About the Marine Sanctuaries Conservation Series

The National Oceanic and Atmospheric Administration administers the National Marine Sanctuary Program. Its mission is to identify, designate, protect and manage the ecological, recreational, research, educational, historical, and aesthetic resources and qualities of nationally significant coastal and marine areas. The existing marine sanctuaries differ widely in their natural and historical resources and include nearshore and open ocean areas ranging in size from less than one to over 5,000 square miles. Protected habitats include rocky coasts, kelp forests, coral reefs, sea grass beds, estuarine habitats, hard and soft bottom habitats, segments of whale migration routes, and shipwrecks.

Because of considerable differences in settings, resources, and threats, each marine sanctuary has a tailored management plan. Conservation, education, research, monitoring and enforcement programs vary accordingly. The integration of these programs is fundamental to marine protected area management. The Marine Sanctuaries Conservation Series reflects and supports this integration by providing a forum for publication and discussion of the complex issues currently facing the National Marine Sanctuary Program. Topics of published reports vary substantially and may include descriptions of educational programs, discussions on resource management issues, and results of scientific research and monitoring projects. The series facilitates integration of natural sciences, socioeconomic and cultural sciences, education, and policy development to accomplish the diverse needs of NOAA's resource protection mandate.

M/V *ELPIS*
Coral Reef Restoration Monitoring Report
Monitoring Events 2004-2007
Florida Keys National Marine Sanctuary
Monroe County, Florida

J. Harold Hudson
Joe Schittone
Jeff Anderson
Erik C. Franklin
Alice Stratton

Florida Keys National Marine Sanctuary
National Marine Sanctuaries Program, National Ocean Service
National Oceanic and Atmospheric Administration

U.S. Department of Commerce
Carlos M. Gutierrez, Secretary

National Oceanic and Atmospheric Administration
VADM Conrad C. Lautenbacher, Jr. (USN-ret.)
Under Secretary of Commerce for Oceans and Atmosphere

National Ocean Service
John H. Dunnigan, Assistant Administrator

Silver Spring, Maryland
March 2008

National Marine Sanctuary Program
Daniel J. Basta, Director

DISCLAIMER

The mention of trade names or commercial products does not constitute endorsement or recommendation for use.

REPORT AVAILABILITY

Electronic copies of this report may be downloaded from the National Marine Sanctuaries Program web site at http://www.sanctuaries.noaa.gov/. Hard copies may be available from the following address:

National Oceanic and Atmospheric Administration
National Marine Sanctuary Program
SSMC4, N/ORM62
1305 East-West Highway
Silver Spring, MD 20910

COVER

Upper left: M/V *Elpis* aground at The Elbow Reef, Florida Keys National Marine Sanctuary. Photo credit: John Halas NMSP/NOAA.

Lower right: School of chub (*Kyphosus* spp.) swimming over limestone boulders covered with naturally-recruited coral colonies, photographed on June 30, 2005, at the M/V *Elpis* restoration site, Florida Keys National Marine Sanctuary. Photo credit: Jeff Anderson NMSP/NOAA.

SUGGESTED CITATION

Hudson, J.H., J. Schittone, J. Anderson, E.C. Franklin, A. Stratton. 2008. M/V *Elpis* Coral Reef Restoration Monitoring Report, Monitoring Events 2004-2007. Florida Keys National Marine Sanctuary Monroe County, Florida. Marine Sanctuaries Conservation Series NMSP-08-03. U.S. Department of Commerce, National Oceanic and Atmospheric Administration, National Marine Sanctuary Program, Silver Spring, MD. 36 pp.

CONTACT

Joe Schittone, corresponding author, at: Joe.Schittone@noaa.gov

ABSTRACT

This document presents the results of the first three monitoring events to track the recovery of a repaired coral reef injured by the M/V *Elpis* vessel grounding incident of November 11, 1989. This grounding occurred within the boundaries of what at the time was designated the Key Largo National Marine Sanctuary (NMS), now designated the Key Largo NMS Existing Management Area within the Florida Keys National Marine Sanctuary (FKNMS). Pursuant to the National Marine Sanctuaries Act (NMSA) 16 U.S.C. 1431 et seq., and the Florida Keys National Marine Sanctuary and Protection Act (FKNMSPA) of 1990, NOAA is the federal trustee for the natural and cultural resources of the FKNMS. Under Section 312 of the NMSA, NOAA has the authority to recover monetary damages for injury, destruction, or loss of Sanctuary resources, and to use the recovered monies to restore injured or lost sanctuary resources within the FKNMS. The restoration monitoring program tracks patterns of biological recovery, determines the success of restoration measures, and assesses the resiliency to environmental and anthropogenic disturbances of the site over time. To evaluate restoration success, reference habitats adjacent to the restoration site are concurrently monitored to compare the condition of restored reef areas with natural coral reef areas unimpacted by the vessel grounding. Restoration of the site was completed September 1995, and thus far three monitoring events have occurred; one in the summer of 2004, one in the summer of 2005, and the latest in the summer of 2007. The monitoring in 2004 was in the nature of a "pilot project," or proof of concept. Only the quantitative results of the 2005 and 2007 monitoring are presented and discussed. Monitoring has consisted of assessment of the structural stability of limestone boulders used in the restoration and comparison of the coral communities on the boulders and reference areas. Corals are divided into Gorgonians, Milleporans, and Scleractinians. Coral densities at the Restored and Reference areas for the 2005 and 2007 events are compared, and it is shown that the densities of all taxa in the Restored area are greater by 2007, though not significantly so. For the Scleractinians, number and percentage of colonies by species, as well as several common biodiversity indices are provided. The greater biodiversity of the Restored area is evidenced. Also, size-class frequency distributions for *Agaricia* spp. (Scleractinia) are presented. These demonstrate the approaching convergence of the Restored and Reference areas in this regard. An inter-annual comparison of densities, within both areas, for all three Orders, is presented. The most noteworthy finding was the relative consistency across time for all taxa in each area. Finally, certain anomalies regarding species settlement patterns are presented.

KEY WORDS

Florida Keys National Marine Sanctuary, coral, grounding, restoration, limestone boulders, monitoring, *Elpis*, Elbow Reef, recruitment, Anthozoa, Hydrozoa, Octocorallia, Hexacorallia, Gorgonacea, Anthoathecata (*Millepora*), Scleractinia

TABLE OF CONTENTS

LIST OF TABLES AND FIGURES

ACKNOWLEDGEMENTS

The National Oceanic and Atmospheric Administration (NOAA) and the Board of Trustees of the Internal Improvement Trust Fund of the State of Florida, ("State of Florida" or "state") are the co-trustees for the natural resources within the FKNMS and, thus, are responsible for mediating the restoration of the damaged marine resources and monitoring the outcome of the restoration actions. The authors would like to express their appreciation to all Florida Department of Environmental Protection employees who participated in the initial response, damage assessment, restoration, and case settlement associated with this vessel grounding. Thanks as well to all reviewers, with a special thanks due to Dr. Dwayne Meadows. All errors remain the authors' own.

INTRODUCTION

This document presents the results of the first three monitoring events to track the recovery of a repaired coral reef injured by the M/V *Elpis* vessel grounding incident of November 11, 1989. This grounding occurred within the boundaries of what at the time was designated the Key Largo National Marine Sanctuary (NMS), now designated the Key Largo NMS Existing Management Area within the Florida Keys National Marine Sanctuary (FKNMS). Pursuant to the National Marine Sanctuaries Act (NMSA) 16 U.S.C. 1431 et seq., and the Florida Keys National Marine Sanctuary and Protection Act (FKNMSPA) of 1990, NOAA is the federal trustee for the natural and cultural resources of the FKNMS. Under Section 312 of the NMSA, NOAA has the authority to recover monetary damages for injury, destruction, or loss of Sanctuary resources, and to use the recovered monies to restore injured or lost sanctuary resources and to monitor their recovery. The restoration monitoring program tracks patterns of biological recovery, determines the success of restoration measures, and assesses the resiliency to environmental and anthropogenic disturbances of the site over time. To evaluate restoration success, reference habitats adjacent to the restoration site are concurrently monitored to compare the condition of restored reef areas with "natural" coral reef areas unimpacted by the vessel grounding or other injury. The monitoring program at the *Elpis* site includes an assessment of the structural stability of installed limestone restoration boulders, and comparison of the recovery of coral populations, to be performed on the following schedule: nine, ten, twelve, and fifteen years after restoration. Restoration of this site was completed in the summer of 1995 with monitoring planned to begin in following years. However, due to staffing and other logistical constraints, the first biological monitoring event for this site, used as a "pilot project" to establish data collection methods, was delayed until August 2004. In June and July 2005, the second monitoring event took place, and in August 2007, the third. This report presents the quantitative results of the latter two monitoring events. An event timeline is presented in Table 1.

Table 1. Event timeline for the M/V *Elpis* grounding site; assessment, restoration, and monitoring.

Event	Date
Vessel Grounding	November 11, 1989
Vessel Removal	November 12, 1989
Injury Assessment: Initial	November 12-December 12, 1989
Injury Assessments: Follow-up	April-June & November-December, 1990
Pre-Construction Survey	June-July 1993
Restoration	June-August, 1995
First Monitoring Event	August, 2004
Second Monitoring Event	June-July, 2005
Third Monitoring Event	August, 2007
Fourth Monitoring Event	Summer 2010

Damage Assessment

[Note: The information in this section was adapted from: Gittings, S., 1991. Reef Coral Destruction at the M/V ELPIS Grounding Site, Key Largo National Marine Sanctuary.]

On November 11, 1989 the M/V Elpis, a 143-meter loaded freighter, ran aground in a reef coral community about 0.4 km (0.25 nautical miles) northeast of the Elbow Reef Light, in 8.5-10 meters of water (Figure 1). Additional injury occurred as result of attempts to "power-off" the reef. The grounding destroyed over 3,000 m^2 of living corals and 878 m^2 of coral reef framework.

The ship was on a heading of 215° when it encountered the sea floor. It came to rest on this heading with the port side of the hull aground. Early the next morning, the ship pivoted approximately 230° counterclockwise and drifted slightly to the northwest, coming to rest on a heading of 345° (Figure 2 and Figure 3). On November 12, the ship was removed from the reef through a combination of towing by a single tug to pivot the M/V *Elpis* bow clockwise (seaward) and the ship's own power.

The grounding of the ship and subsequent attempts to free it resulted in significant injury to the reef substrate and resident marine organisms. Approximately 94 percent of the coral colonies, and 93 percent of the total coral cover in the grounding area, as well as numerous sponges and sea fans at the site, were destroyed. Moreover, virtually all survivors showed evidence of injury caused by the grounding. The injuries ranged from superficial scraping of the reef surface, toppling and fracturing of large coral heads, severe cracking and excavating of the reef framework structure, and burial by resulting sediments and rubble. Attempts by the vessel to extricate itself caused "blowholes" (excavations caused by high-revving propellers) in the reef's surface and the displaced material from these blowholes accumulated as berms (linear mounds) up to 1 m high and tens of meters long (Figure 4).

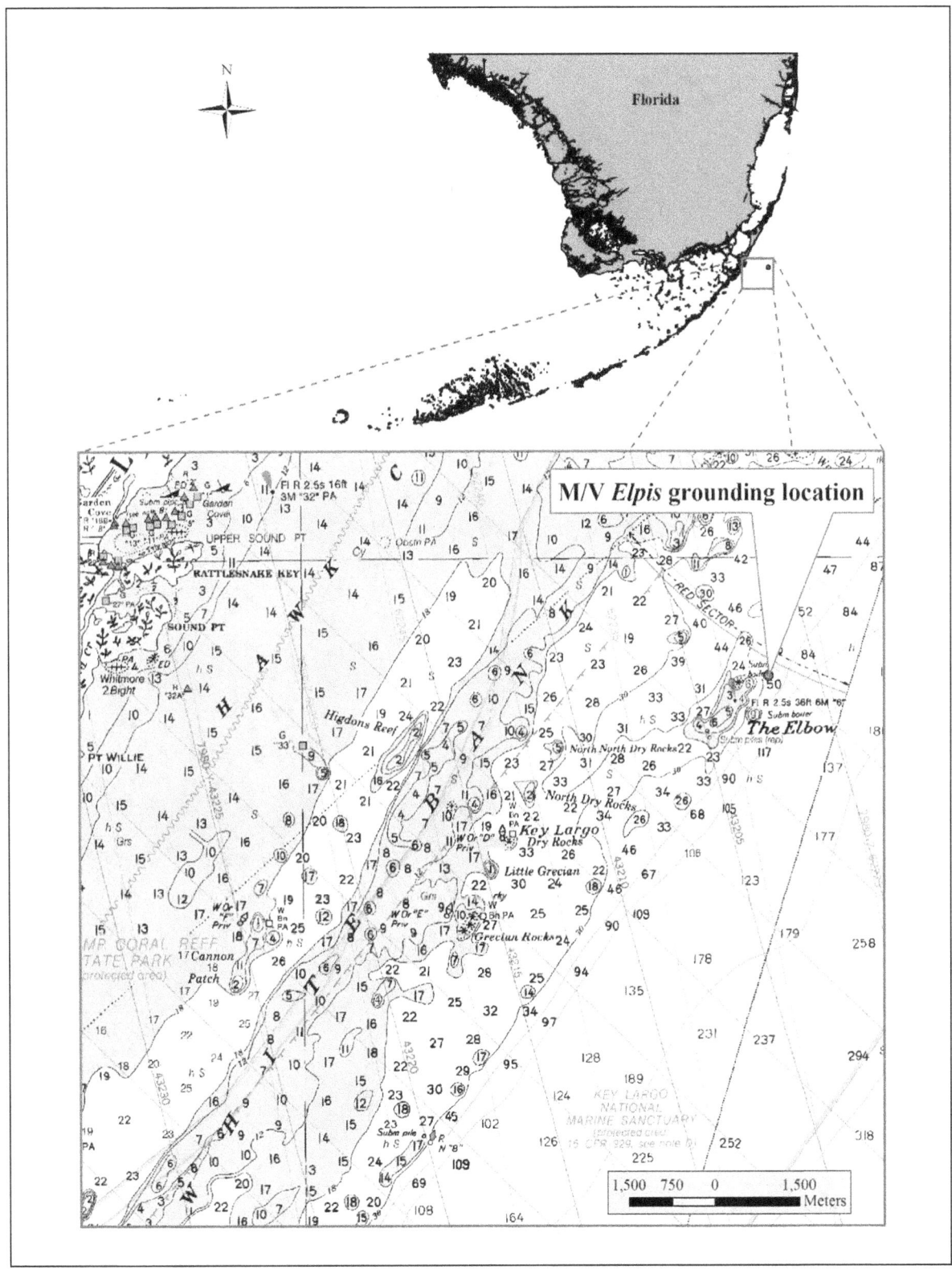

Figure 1. Location (shown on NOAA Chart 11462) that the M/V *Elpis* ran aground at The Elbow Reef on November 11, 1989.

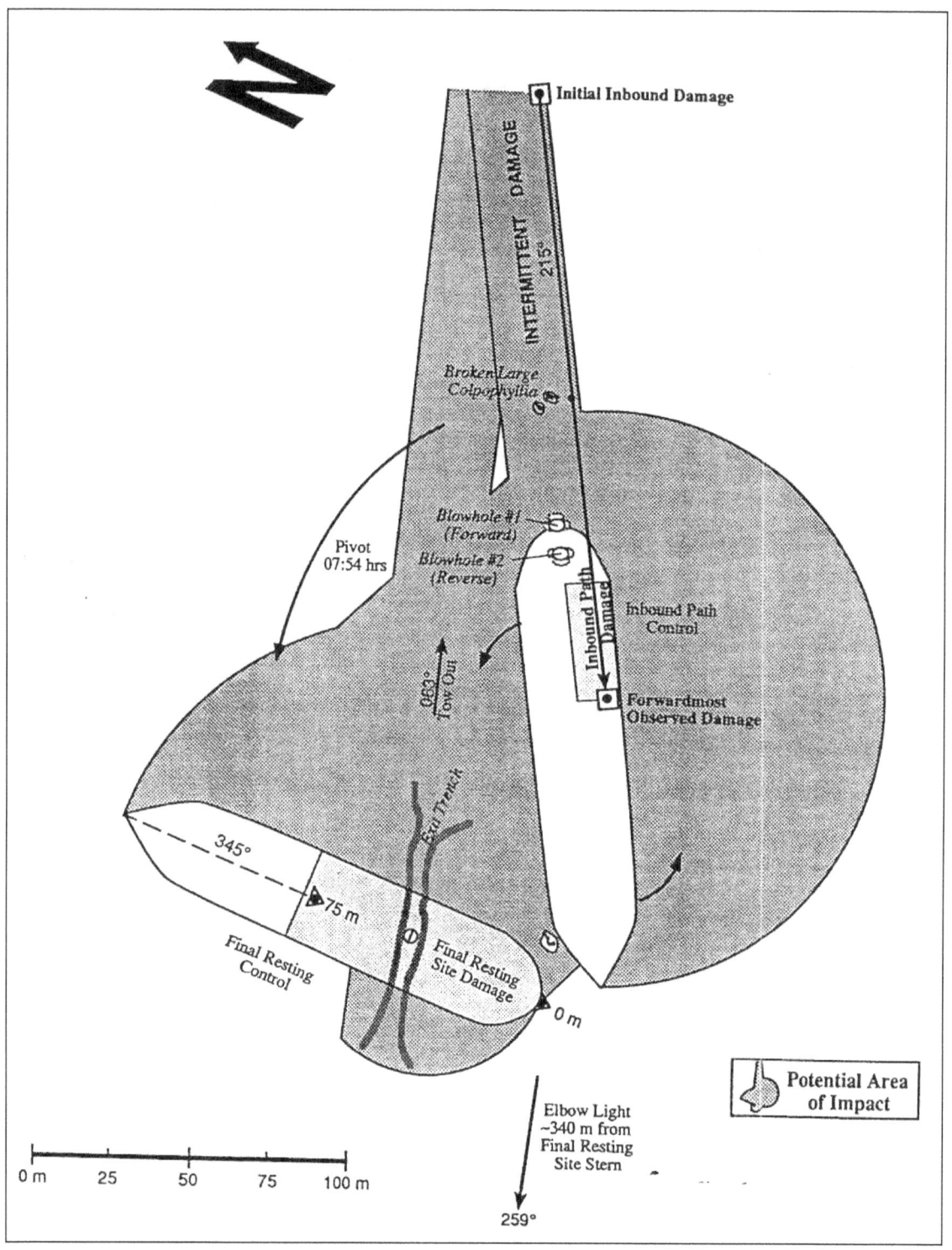

Figure 2. Diagram of the grounding site of the M/V *Elpis*, indicating the location of the grounded ship on the inbound path, and on its final resting site after pivoting and drifting off the inbound path. Shaded region indicated the areas of bottom potentially affected by the ship (Gittings 1991).

4

Figure 3. M/V *Elpis* aground at The Elbow Reef. Notice stream of white sediment emerging from the stern of the vessel (photo credit: Florida Keys National Marine Sanctuary).

Figure 4. Overturned *Colpophyllia natans* colony (left) and berm/blowhole material (right) resulting from the grounding and attempts to extricate the vessel (Photo credits: Florida Keys National Marine Sanctuary).

Based on surveys from natural hard-bottom communities in the vicinity, the M/V *Elpis* grounding impacted a coral reef community dominated by soft corals and small hard corals. These groups totaled approximately 15 colonies/m² and percent cover averaged 10%. The most abundant soft corals were the genus *Pseudopterogorgia*, most being *P. americana*. Other common soft corals included *Pterogorgia citrina*, *Briareum asbestinum*, and *Erythropodium caribaeorum*.

The six most abundant hard corals in the nearby reference areas, from most to least abundant, included: *Favia fragum*, *Agaricia* spp., *Dichocoenia stokesii*, *Porites* spp., *Siderastrea* spp. and *Montastraea annularis* complex. Nearly all hard corals were small, as reflected by their percent cover of less than 2%.

5

Fire corals, represented by the genus *Millepora*, mostly *M. alcicornis*, accounted for roughly 10% of all coral cover and 18% of all coral colonies in the nearby reference areas. Again, the low relative percent cover reflects the colonies' small average size.

Although abundant in certain zones on other Florida Keys' reefs, neither upright sponges nor colonial anemones (*Palythoa* spp.) appeared to contribute significantly to the benthic assemblage at the M/V *Elpis* grounding site.

A settlement between NOAA and the responsible parties was agreed to in July 1991. The damages received from the responsible parties were allocated to repayment of response and damage assessment costs and for future restoration of the site. Restoration undertaken in 1995 was planned by National Marine Sanctuary Program (NMSP) headquarters and FKNMS staff, in collaboration with marine engineers from the commercial firm of Olsen Associates, Inc., and implemented by Team Land and Development, Inc. along with FKNMS staff.

Coral Reef Restoration

[Note: The information in this section was adapted from: Bodge, K. 1996. Engineering Summary Report: Structural Restoration of the *M/V Alec Owen Maitland* and *M/V Elpis* Vessel Grounding Sites: Florida Keys National Marine Sanctuary. Report prepared for: NOAA/Office of Ocean Resources Conservation and Assessment.]

The goal of the M/V *Elpis* restoration project was to re-create a stable foundation that closely emulated the adjacent natural seabed to foster recruitment of coral colonies. Because of the size, irregular shape, and contour of the blowholes, as well as the depth of the restoration site, the use of boulders was selected as the restoration method (Bodge and Creed 1993) compared to the use of prefabricated concrete armor units at the much shallower M/V *Alec Owen Maitland* site. (see the *Maitland* restoration project web site for more information: http://www.darrp.noaa.gov/southeast/maitland/index.html). Rubble (primarily *Acropora cervicornis* rubble) and small rocks from the nearby berms were used to fill the blowholes to the specified level. Natural coral rocks larger than 2 ft. diameter present in these berms were set aside for later use. Quarried marine limestone boulders averaging 4.25 ft. diameter (Bodge 1994) were individually placed on the fill, and the large natural coral rocks were intermixed (Figure 5). All boulders were placed such that they were in contact with each other; interlocking to form a compact mass. Oolitic carbonate sand imported from the Bahamas was placed from a barge to fill the interstitial spaces of the reef rubble and boulders within the filled blowholes.

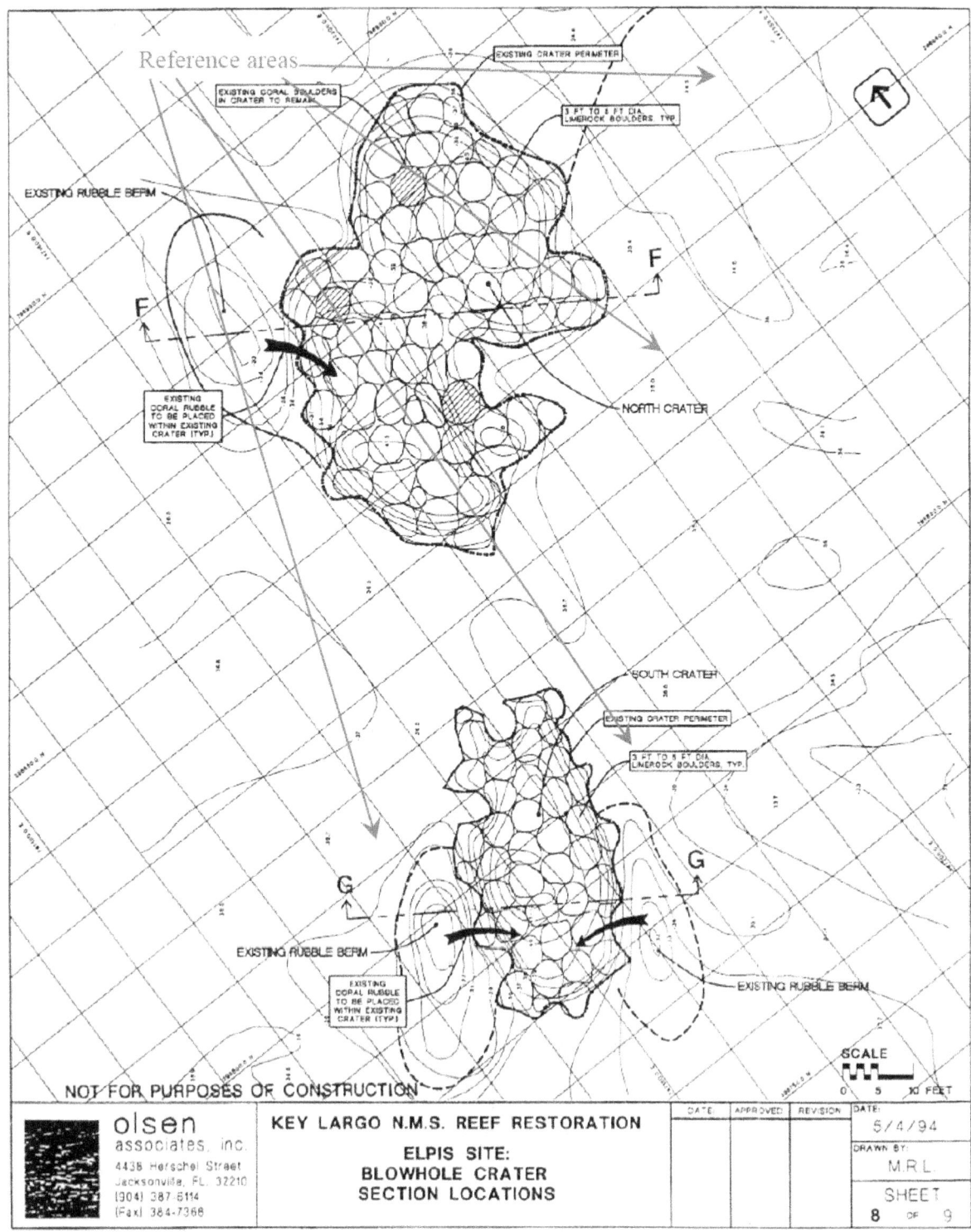

Figure 5. Schematic diagram of restoration area depicting how blowholes will be filled with boulders along with approximate location of Reference sampling areas.

Figure 6. Restoration of the blowhole craters – Divers installing quarried limestone boulders (top row) and the completed restoration (bottom row) (photo credits: Harold Hudson NMSP/NOAA).

Restoration Monitoring

The purpose of the NMSP coral restoration monitoring program is to evaluate the success of trustee actions in achieving restoration goals and to determine if remedial measures are needed. For a grounding site such as the M/V *Elpis*, the evaluation of restoration efforts involves the identification of appropriate success criteria and the design and implementation of a sampling and analysis plan. A list of success criteria measures for structural and functional aspects of coral reef restoration as well as a framework for monitoring activities has been identified by NOAA (Thayer et al. 2003).

The guiding hypotheses for the evaluation of the restoration site reflect the efficacy of the restoration techniques and the condition of the site relative to reference habitats. The monitoring program addresses whether the chosen restoration methods are effective, and whether and when the site can be considered restored. The monitoring program for the M/V *Elpis* site is evaluating the structural stability of restored habitat and coral population parameters of the restoration site.

The structural integrity of the restoration site was evaluated with the following questions:

Is the attachment of the reef restoration boulders to the substrate stable?

In addition, the biological condition of the restoration site was evaluated with the following question:

Is there a difference in coral colony densities, biodiversity, and other population parameters between the Restored area and the Reference areas?

The monitoring program was also designed to detect significant changes in coral colonies on the reef restoration boulders, versus the Reference areas, as a result of external events, such as major storms.

METHODOLOGY

MONITORING EVENTS

The first monitoring survey was conducted on August 16, 19, & 24, 2004. This first survey was used as a "pilot project" for data collection methods at the site. On June 30, and July 1, & 6, 2005, the *Elpis* restoration site was again monitored, and on August 3, 9, & 14, 2007, the site was monitored for the third time. Monitoring was conducted using SCUBA from a small vessel (6.4 m). Prior to the June 2005 monitoring events, the eyes of three powerful hurricanes passed within 250 kilometers of the restoration site; Charley in late August, and Jeanne and Frances in September 2004. Each consisted of winds approximating 175-195 kph at the time of closest approach to the restoration site. The possible confounding effects of these hurricanes, if any, are unknown, since definitive monitoring was not done in 2004. In 2005, hurricane Dennis made its closest approach between the June and July portions of the 2005 monitoring event, at similar distance and wind speeds as noted for the 2004 storms. In addition, after the July 2005 monitoring, hurricanes Katrina, Rita, and Wilma passed within 175 km of the site. At the time of closest approach, Katrina and Rita had winds of about 130 kph. Wilma had winds of approximately 205 kph, but was over land (SW Florida) at the time. No monitoring of the site was conducted between July 2005 and the 2007 monitoring, and thus the possible confounding effects of these hurricanes, if any, are likewise unknown. However, no visually or tactilely perceptible damage was observed at the restoration site, after either the 2004 or 2005 storms.

Field Methods

Tactile and visual assessments were performed to evaluate the physical stability of the reef restoration. To determine the biological condition of the site, *in situ* observations were recorded; digital images and digital videos were also taken. The "Reference" area was adjacent to the restoration site (Figure 5). In both 2005 and 2007, within the "Restored" area, 12 haphazardly selected boulders were surveyed for biological variables of interest as described in the *Biological Classifications* section (following). In both years, a similar number of haphazardly selected "boulders" were examined in the immediately adjacent, but unimpacted, Reference area. These boulders actually consisted of natural reef outcroppings, selected on the basis of similarity in size and shape to the restoration boulders, as estimated according to the "pilot project" conducted at this site in 2004.

Oblique digital photographs were taken of each boulder in the restored area, selected coral colonies of interest, and the overall landscape/topography of the surveyed areas. Underwater digital images were collected with an Olympus C-5050 digital camera in a Light & Motion Tetra 5050 underwater housing and digital videos were collected with a Sony DCR-DVD200 video camera in an Amphibico QuickView DVD underwater housing.

Photo Analysis

No quantitative analysis of photographic images was conducted. The images were used to qualitatively record the state of the restoration site in general and particular items of interest. Digital images were edited with Adobe Photoshop versions 7 and CS2 (Adobe 2002 and 2005). Image edits included color hue changes to bring-out natural colors, brightness changes to compensate for original exposure, and sharpness changes to enhance image focus.

Biological Classifications

The majority of the benthos visible was comprised of three Orders of the Phylum Cnidaria, and most of the comparisons presented are at the Order level. Present were members of the Order Anthoathecata in the Class Hydrozoa (specimens were solely of one Genus in the Family Milliporidae and henceforth referred to by the name of that Genus—*Millepora*), and the Orders Gorgonacea and Scleractinia of the Subclasses Octocorallia and Hexacorallia respectively (Class Anthozoa). Scleractinians were further divided into species for various analytical purposes.

Although not included in this analysis, numerous vagile fauna were observed on the restoration site, including those pictured in Figure 7. The habitat value of the restoration boulders for vagile fauna was likely enhanced by the colonization of sessile fauna.

Figure 7. Fauna living in and around *Elpis* restoration site. Top row: chub (*Kyphosus* spp.) (left), neon gobies (*Gobiosoma oceanops*) on *Montastraea faveolata* (right). Bottom row: French grunt (*Haemulon flavolineatum*), bluestriped grunt (*Haemulon sciurus*), and porkfish (*Anisotremus virginicus*) (left), Christmas tree worm (*Spirobranchus giganteus*) (right) (photo credits: Jeff Anderson NMSP/NOAA).

Data Analysis

Again, using the 2004 pilot project as a guide, it was determined that the best method to convert the boulders into a unit of standard measure (m^2 surface area) was the model that follows. It was

11

determined that the surface area of the boulder shapes was most closely approximated by considering each as if it was an ellipsoidal right cylinder, standing on end. Measures of the lengths of the major and minor axis, and the height of each, were obtained and used (after subtracting for the bottom "face" of the cylinder, resting on the substrate) to calculate surface area, according to the formula: $2\pi*(a+b)/4*h + \pi*a/2*b/2$; where a, b, & h, are the lengths of the major and minor axes and height, respectively. (Actually this is not a perfectly correct formula for the surface area; however, it tremendously simplifies computational effort, yields a result always within $\approx$ 2% of the true figure, that of the frustum of an oblique cylinder, and the skew is always in the same direction.) Doing so yielded similar surface areas; after randomly eliminating one boulder from the 2005 reference area, total surface areas for both sites, over both years, varied only between 51 and 52.5 m^2, with the restoration area being $\approx$ 0.75 to 1 m^2 *less* in each year.

Data analysis was performed on a Dell PC with InStat$^{®}$ version 3.0 (GraphPad 2003), Prism 5 for Windows (GraphPad 2007), and Microsoft$^{®}$ Excel 2003 software. Descriptive statistics were generated for samples collected among the restoration and reference areas, along with various analytic statistics for comparative purposes.

In the 2005 density analyses, for the Gorgonian and Scleractinian populations a square root transformation was performed to meet Gaussian distribution requirements, permitting two-tailed *t* test comparisons (For all data, whenever transformation was deemed necessary [as per Kolmogorov-Smirnov normality testing] since the underlying data arose from enumerative counts evidencing Poisson distributions, it proceeded by way of square root transformations.). For the Milleporans, no transformation was required, but the *t* test was conducted by way of Welch's correction, to account for the heteroscedasticity of the data set.

For the 2007 analyses, for the Scleractinians, the data could not be rendered Gaussian by transformation; thus the non-parametric Mann-Whitney *U* test was used. The Gorgonian corals evidenced a normal distribution with no need for transformation or correction. The Milleporan data was transformed, there was homogeneity of variance, and the *t* test was performed without need for correction.

For both years, common biodiversity indices were calculated for the Scleractinian populations. Additionally, size-class frequency distributions are shown for the only coral taxa present in sufficient numbers to allow a meaningful classification (*Agaricia* spp.).

Finally, some inter-annual comparisons between 2005 and 2007 are made for densities of all Orders, in both areas. In the restored areas, for the Scleractinians, the data could not be normalized, and the comparison proceeded by a Mann-Whitney *U* test. For the Gorgonians, a *t* test was conducted with no transformation or correction. For the Milleporans, transformation was required, but no correction.

RESULTS

Structural Integrity

The 2004 monitoring occurred 9 years after the restoration, at which time the stability and surface of all restoration boulders were found to be visually and tactilely sound. The boulders were found in place with a stable attachment to the substrate.

Biological Condition

The biological recovery of the restoration site was progressing. Macroalgae, crustose coralline algae, soft, and hard corals were all recruiting to the restoration boulders. For a more comprehensive set of boulder photographs tracking their biological condition over time, please see the APPENDIX. No quantitative results from this pilot project monitoring survey are presented.

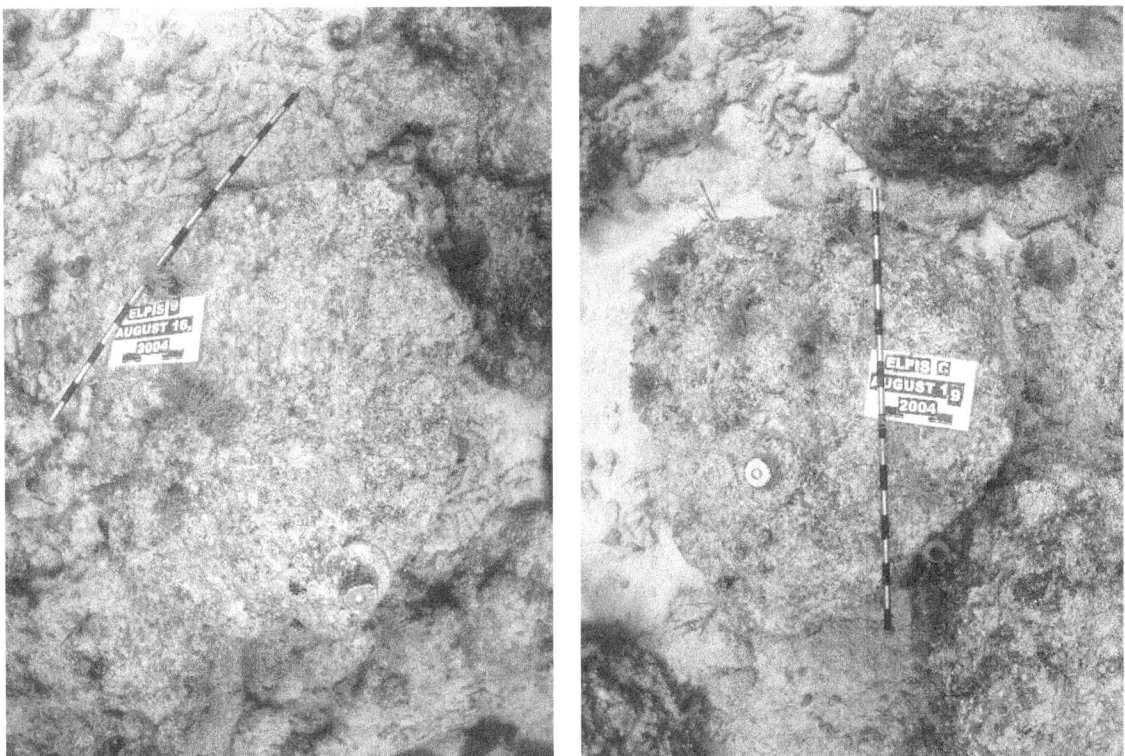

Figure 8. Restoration boulders showing biological condition 9 years after installation (photo credits: Jeff Anderson NMSP/NOAA).

13

SECOND MONITORING EVENT (JUNE-JULY 2005)

Structural Integrity

The 2005 monitoring occurred 10 years after the restoration, at which time the stability and surface of all restoration boulders were found to be visually and tactilely sound. Despite the close passage of three hurricanes between the 2004 pilot survey and 2005 monitoring event (see METHODOLOGY); the boulders were found in place with a stable attachment to the substrate.

Biological Condition

The biological recovery of the restoration site continued to progress. Macroalgae, crustose coralline algae, soft, and hard corals were all recruiting to the restoration boulders (Figure 9 and Figure 10). For a more comprehensive set of boulder photographs tracking their biological condition over time, please see the APPENDIX. For the three Orders surveyed in 2005, the data yielded the densities shown in Figure 11.

Figure 9. Representative restoration boulders showing biological condition 10 years after installation (photo credits: Jeff Anderson NMSP/NOAA).

Figure 10. Representative benthic organisms surveyed on the *Elpis* restoration boulders. Starting from top left: *Agaricia* sp., *Montastraea cavernosa*, *Psuedopterogorgia* spp., *Diploria labyrinthiformis*, *Porites porites*, *Millepora alcicornis* (photo credits: Jeff Anderson NMSP/NOAA).

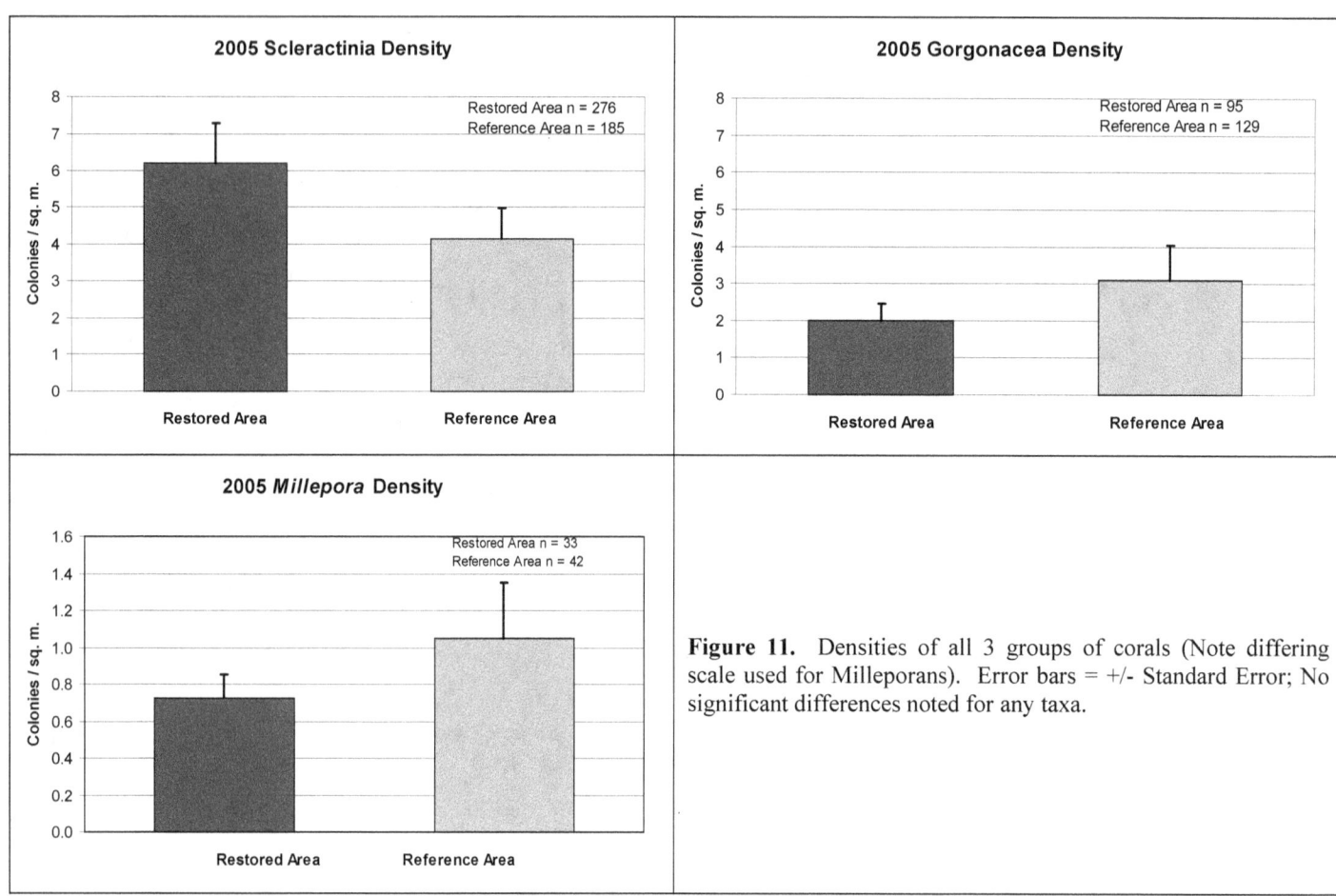

Figure 11. Densities of all 3 groups of corals (Note differing scale used for Milleporans). Error bars = +/- Standard Error; No significant differences noted for any taxa.

In addition to the density data, information regarding species identification (or in some cases only to Genus level) was gathered for Scleractinians. Those data are presented in Table 2, immediately followed by Table 3, which gives several standard biodiversity index calculations.

Table 2. Number of Scleractinian colonies, by species, surveyed in 2005 at the *Elpis* restoration site.

Species	Restored area	Reference area
Agaricia spp.	55	59
Colpophylia natans	0	1
Dichocoenia stokesii	10	1
Diploria labyrinthiformis	2	0
Diploria spp.	3	3
Eusimilia fastigiata	0	1
Favia fragum	11	0
Madracis spp.	0	32
Meandrina meandrites	1	0
Montastraea annularis	1	0
Montastraea cavernosa	17	5
Montastraea faveolata	0	26
Mycetophyllia spp.	0	1
Porites astreoides	49	18
Porites porites	36	27
Siderastrea radians	21	0
Siderastrea siderea	60	9
Solenastrea bournoni	2	0
Stephanocoenia intersepta	2	2
Unknown	6	0
Total	**276**	**185**

Table 3. Common biodiversity indices of the 2005 Scleractinian colony population at the *Elpis* restoration site.

Name of Index (along with formulas)	Restored area	Reference area
Species Richness: $S = \#$	15	13
Simpson's index: $D = \Sigma(P_i^2)$	0.149	0.186
Shannon-Weiner: $H = -\Sigma(P_i \log[P_i])$	2.122	1.925
Evenness: $E = H/\log(S)$	0.784	0.750

Information regarding the relative proportions of Scleractinians present in both the Restored and Reference areas is additionally presented in Figure 12.

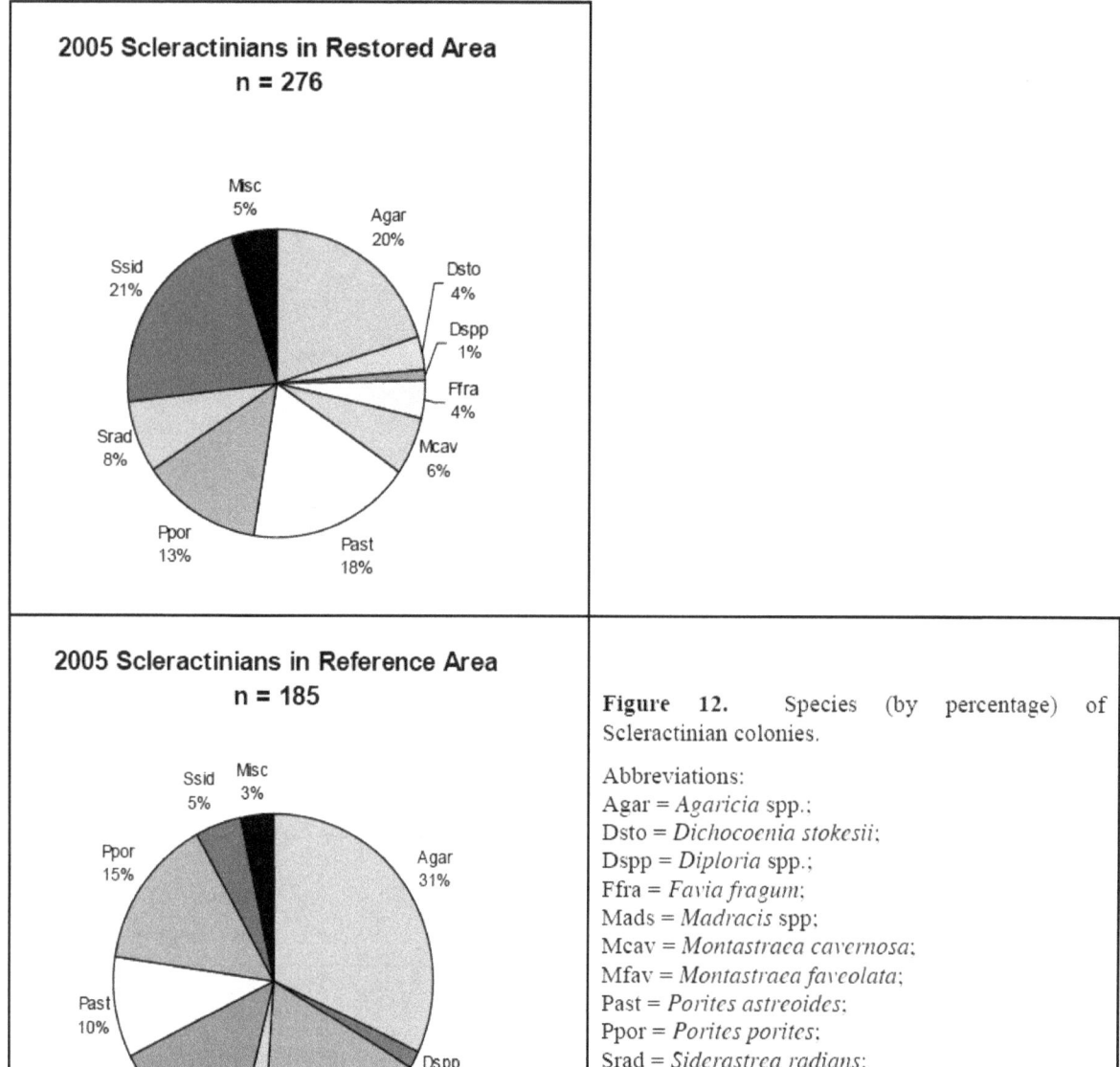

Figure 12. Species (by percentage) of Scleractinian colonies.

Abbreviations:
Agar = *Agaricia* spp.;
Dsto = *Dichocoenia stokesii*;
Dspp = *Diploria* spp.;
Ffra = *Favia fragum*;
Mads = *Madracis* spp;
Mcav = *Montastraea cavernosa*;
Mfav = *Montastraea faveolata*;
Past = *Porites astreoides*;
Ppor = *Porites porites*;
Srad = *Siderastrea radians*;
Ssid = *Siderastrea siderea*;
Misc = Unknown, Unidentified, and any species with fewer than three colonies, lumped together.

Finally, size-class frequency distributions were ascertained for the only coral with sufficient numbers to make such calculations meaningful, that being *Agaricia* spp. The graphs depicting the distribution are shown in Figure 13.

18

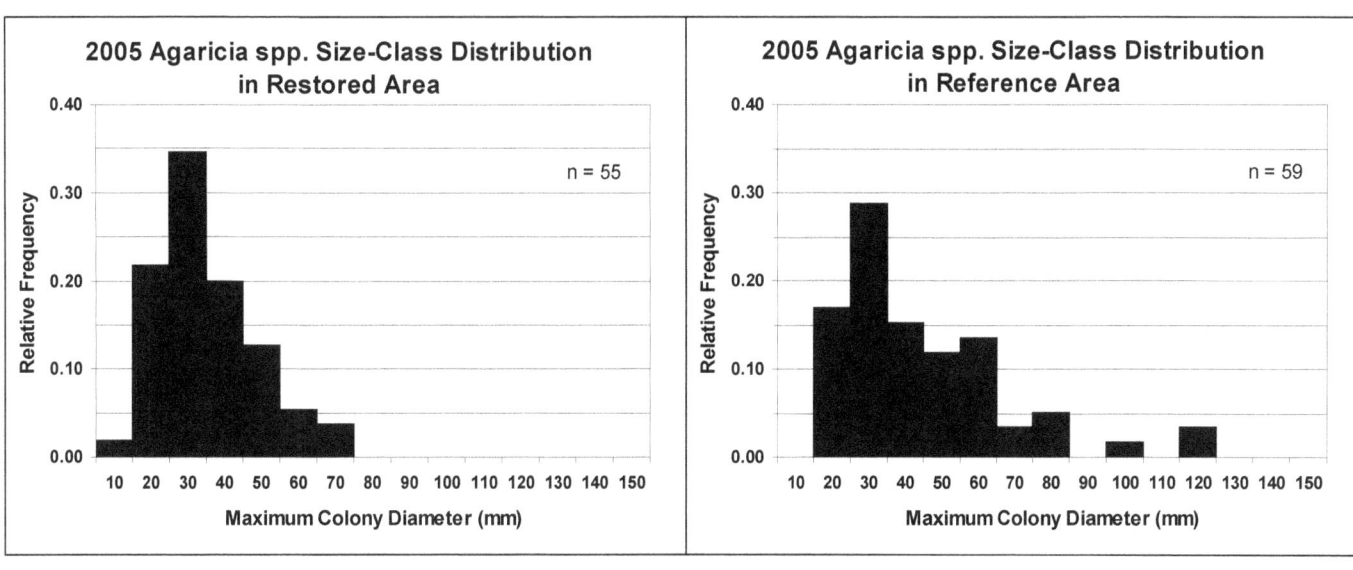

Figure 13. Size-class frequency distribution of *Agaricia* spp. in the Restored and Reference areas in 2005.

THIRD MONITORING EVENT (JULY-SEPTEMBER 2007)

Structural Integrity

Despite the near passage of four hurricanes during the 2005 storm season (see METHODOLOGY), the stability and surface of all reef restoration boulders were again found to be visually and tactilely sound.

Biological Condition

The biological recovery of the restoration site continued to progress. Macroalgae, crustose coralline algae, soft, and hard corals were all still present on the restoration boulders. For a more comprehensive set of boulder photographs tracking their biological condition over time, please see the APPENDIX. For the three Orders surveyed in 2007, the data yielded the densities shown in Figure 14.

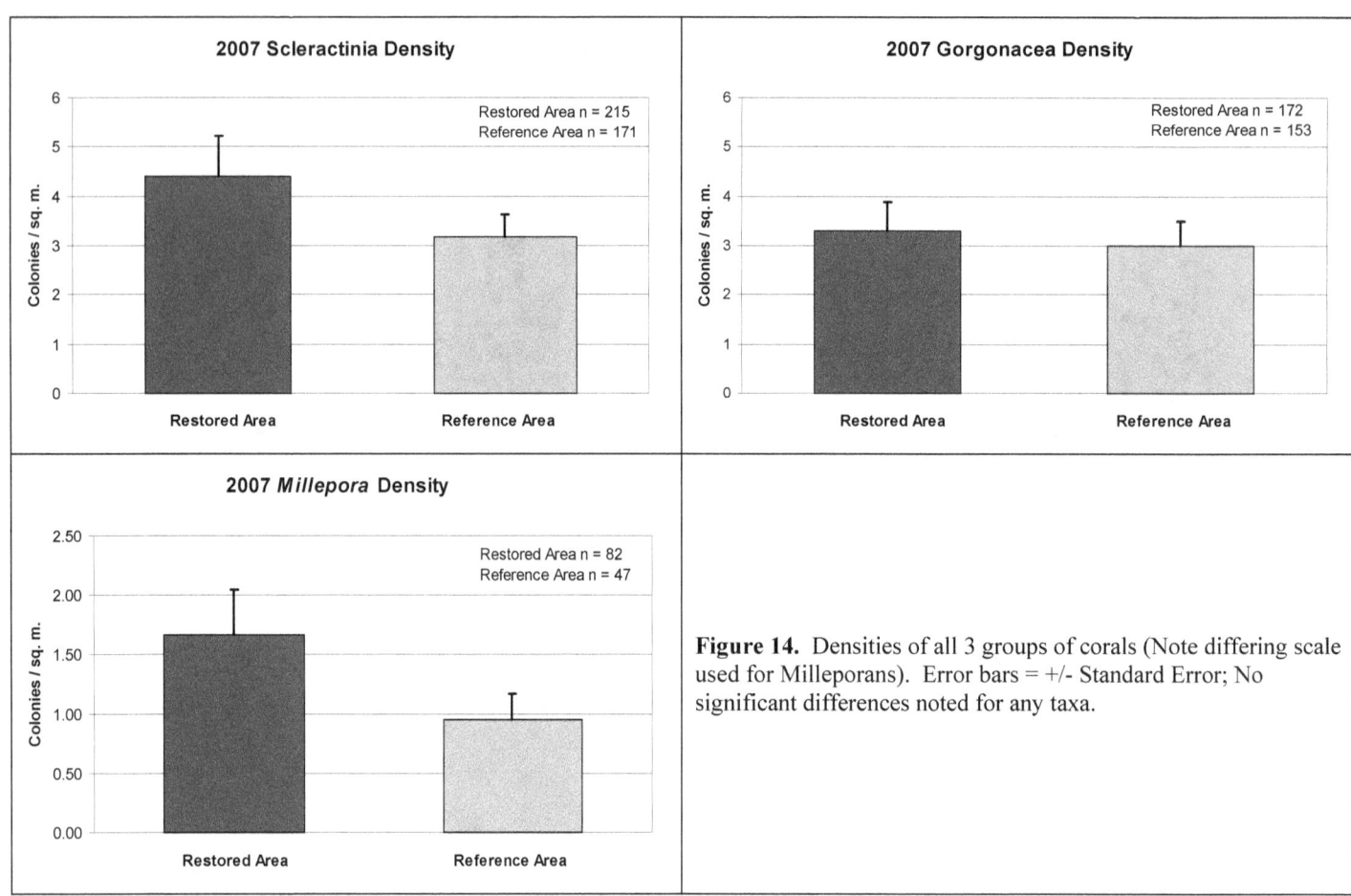

Figure 14. Densities of all 3 groups of corals (Note differing scale used for Milleporans). Error bars = +/- Standard Error; No significant differences noted for any taxa.

In addition to the density data, information regarding species identification (or in some cases only to Genus level) was gathered for Scleractinians. Those data are presented in Table 4, immediately followed by Table 5 which gives several biodiversity index calculations

Table 4. Number of Scleractinian colonies, by species, surveyed in 2007 at the *Elpis* restoration site.

Species	Restored area	Reference area
Agaricia spp.	40	83
Diploria spp.	2	3
Dichocoenia stokesii	8	0
Favia fragum	27	1
Madracis spp.	0	34
Montastraea annularis	1	0
Montastraea cavernosa	5	2
Mussa angulosa	0	1
Porites astreoides	46	22
Porites porites	36	19
Siderastrea radians	9	0
Siderastrea siderea	35	5
Solenastrea bournoni	1	0
Stephanocoenia intersepta	3	1
Unknown	2	0
Total	**215**	**171**

Table 5. Common biodiversity indices of the 2007 Scleractinian colony population at the *Elpis* restoration site.

Name of Index (along with formulas)	Restored area	Reference area
Species Richness: S = #	13	10
Simpson's index: $D = \Sigma(P_i^2)$	0.155	0.305
Shannon-Weiner: $H = -\Sigma(P_i\log[P_i])$	2.038	1.495
Evenness: $E = H/\log(S)$	0.794	0.650

The relative proportions of Scleractinians present in both the Restored and Reference areas are presented in Figure 15.

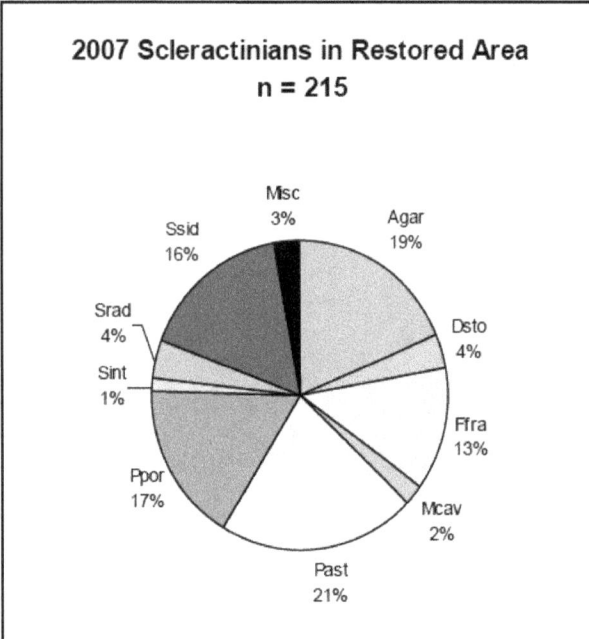

2007 Scleractinians in Restored Area
n = 215

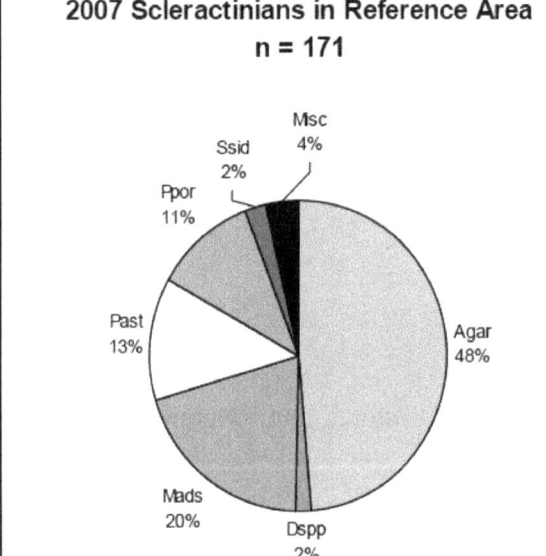

2007 Scleractinians in Reference Area
n = 171

Figure 15. Species (by percentage) of Scleractinian colonies.

Abbreviations:
Agar = *Agaricia* spp.;
Dsto = *Dichocoenia stokesii*;
Dspp = *Diploria* spp.;
Ffra = *Favia fragum*;
Mads = *Madracis* spp;
Mcav = *Montastraea cavernosa*;
Past = *Porites astreoides*;
Ppor = *Porites porites*;
Sint = *Stephanocoenia intersepta*;
Srad = *Siderastrea radians*;
Ssid = *Siderastrea siderea*;
Misc = Unknown, Unidentified, and any species with fewer than three colonies, lumped together.

As for the previous years, the 2007 size-class frequency distributions were ascertained for the only coral with sufficient numbers to make such calculations meaningful, again *Agaricia* spp. The graphs depicting the distribution are shown in Figure 16.

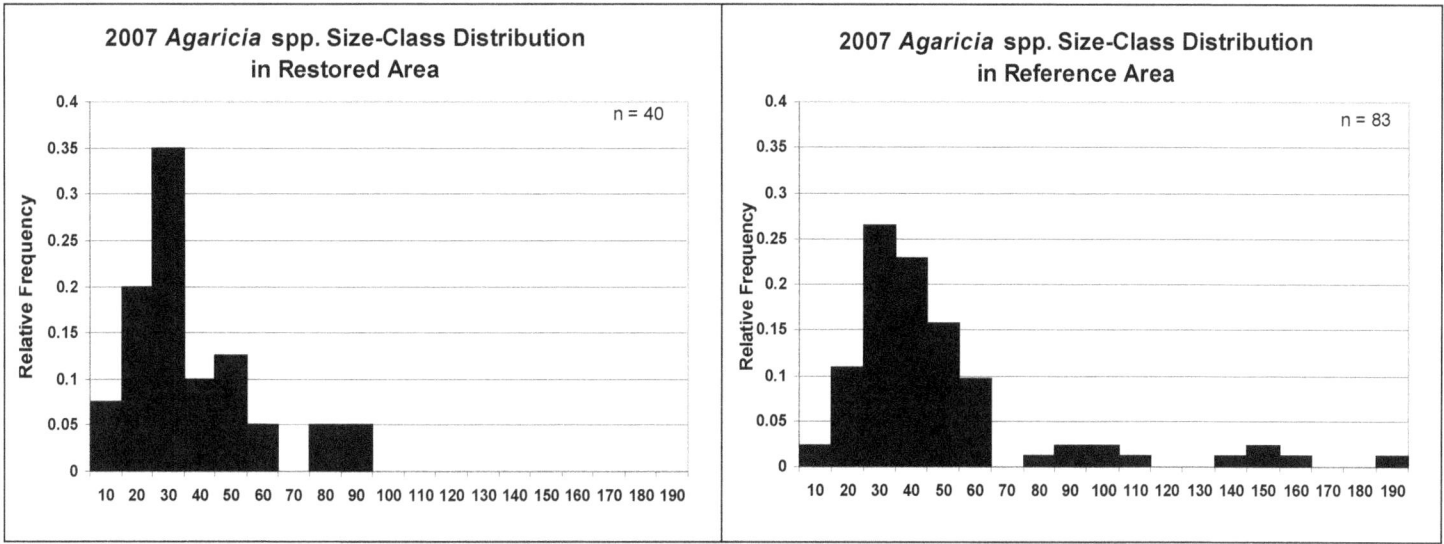

Figure 16. Size-class frequency distribution of *Agaricia* spp. in the Restored and Reference areas in 2007.

In addition to examining data for individual years, some inter-annual comparisons were made. Scatterplots of the densities follow.

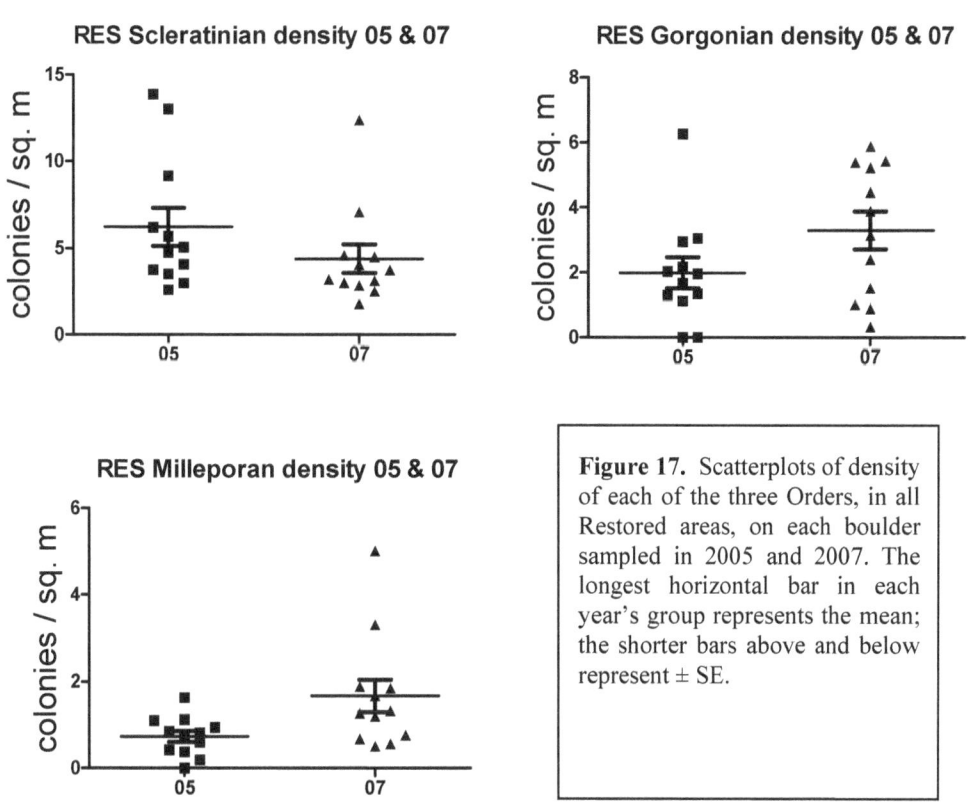

Figure 17. Scatterplots of density of each of the three Orders, in all Restored areas, on each boulder sampled in 2005 and 2007. The longest horizontal bar in each year's group represents the mean; the shorter bars above and below represent ± SE.

23

For the Restored area Scleractinians, densities were similar for 2005 and 2007. While they appeared to slightly decrease in 2007, no significant difference was detected.

For the Gorgonians, mean densities were similar for 2005 and 2007 with, however, several suspected outliers in each data set. While densities appeared to increase in 2007, no significant difference was noted, regardless of whether or not the outlier data points are included in the analysis.

For the Milleporans, densities showed an increase from 2005 to 2007. The difference was significant ($p = 0.0155$).

Finally, plots for the Reference areas, for all taxa, for both years, are presented below. No significant difference for any taxa was noted.

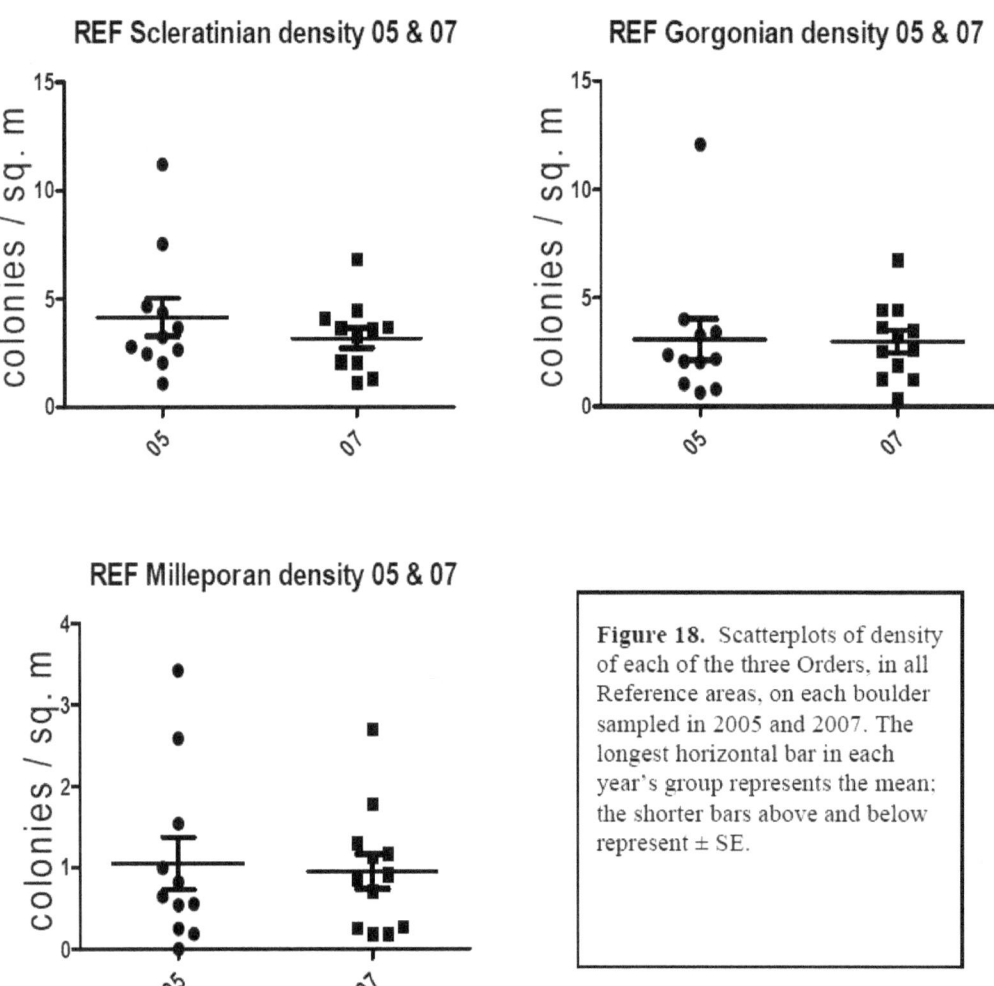

Figure 18. Scatterplots of density of each of the three Orders, in all Reference areas, on each boulder sampled in 2005 and 2007. The longest horizontal bar in each year's group represents the mean; the shorter bars above and below represent ± SE.

DISCUSSION

The results of the 2005 and 2007 *Elpis* restoration monitoring surveys indicate a gradual but definitive recovery of a coral community in the Restored area. However, several points should be kept in mind while reviewing results, primarily the duration and scope of the monitoring program. Regarding duration, it is important to remember that this report reflects only the preliminary stages of a longer term (10-year) monitoring program. The development of coral communities is well-known to be a long-term (decadal) process, so NMSP does not expect to be able to make definitive conclusions about the success of the *Elpis* restoration at this stage. However, the presence of numerous coral recruits 10 years after installation provides a good indication that the structural stability offered by the restoration boulders are already providing suitable substrate and environment for the ongoing development of reef habitat. As for the scope of the monitoring program, it should be reiterated that this monitoring effort is tracking only some aspects of coral restoration, namely, stability, recruitment, biodiversity, and size distribution.

For the 2005 density data (Figure 11) the Restored area Scleractinians seemed to be recruiting well, with total colony numbers being 6.2 col./m^2, vs. 4.1 col./m^2 in the Reference area. Gorgonians and Milleporans appeared to fare a bit more poorly. The densities of the former in the Restoration and Reference areas respectively, was 2.0 and 3.1 col./m^2; while for the latter they were 0.7 vs. 1.1 col./m^2. However, in none of the three Orders did the differences prove significant.

Table 2 and Table 3 show a greater species richness, biodiversity, and number of colonies of Scleractinians in the Restored area, and proportions are depicted graphically in Figure 12. The discrepancies noted in biodiversity values are not great. The only distinction that proved quite large (in terms of absolute numbers) was for the Genus *Siderastrea*, with 81 colonies in the Restored area and only 9 in the Reference. This may have important implications that bode well for the restoration, since the species is one of the few large, framework-builder, broadcasting species to recruit in substantial numbers in the Restored area. An even more dramatic difference—in percentage terms—was presented by the Genus *Madracis*; while the Restored area contained none (0), the Reference area held 32 colonies.

The size-class frequency distribution of *Agaricia* spp. shown in Figure 13 gives rise to some interesting observations. The figure reveals that, at least for this Genus, the distribution in the Restored area is converging with that demonstrated by the Reference area, as one might expect 10 years after a restoration. The 30-40 mm size class in each comprised about one third of both populations, though the larger (60 mm and above) colonies still had a considerable lead in the Reference area, where they made up 27% of the population, versus 9% in the Restored area. This is not surprising, the growth rate of *Agaricia* spp. being moderately slow at about 10 mm/yr. in diameter linear extension (Box and Mumby 2007).

Looking at the 2007 data, the Restored area appeared to be faring better in all three Order categories, although again, the differences weren't significant (Figure 14). For Scleractinians, the Restoration area contained 4.4 col./m^2, while the Reference area held 3.2 col./m^2. The density of Gorgonians was nearly identical, at 3.3 and 3.0 col./m². For Milleporans, the respective figures are 1.7 vs. 1.0 col./m².

Table 4 and Table 5 reveal that the restored area is "widening its lead" in the species richness and biodiversity arena. The taxa noted above continued to display the same general preference pattern. This time *Siderastrea* had 44 colonies in the Restored area versus 5 in the Reference, while—practically identically with the 2005 data—*Madracis* showed 0 in the Restored area and 34 in the Reference. These apparent differences in site preferences by Genus are unexplained. It should be remembered that the settlement surfaces are similar, both in terms of material and configuration. Both are composed of limestone "rock" outcroppings; the Restoration area boulders are relict reef quarried in the Keys—having undergone no treatment—while of course the Reference area is extant reef. Similarly, they are of the same approximate shape, size, and topographic complexity. Nor can what is commonly referred to as a necessary period of underwater "conditioning" have been a factor; by the time of these monitoring events in 2005 and 2007, the restoration boulders had been down 10 and 12 years respectively. Perhaps the reason had to do with taxa successional processes, though this explanation is speculative. It seems unlikely that *Siderastrea* would be replaced by *Madracis* in any event (Lang et al. 1992). (Should any reader have thoughts on the differential recruitment preferences by Genus, contact with the corresponding author would be appreciated.)

Equally noteworthy is the overall species mix. At the 2007 monitoring event *Agaricia* spp. made up almost half the total colonies in the Reference area (Figure 15). Obviously then, biodiversity and evenness in the area dropped considerably (Table 5).

The Agaricid size-class frequency distribution for 2007 (Figure 16) was rendered somewhat less robust, in that in this year there were only 40 colonies in the Restored area to be classified. Nevertheless, the pattern noted above can generally be said to have continued. In fact, for the larger size categories (≥ 60 mm) the gap appeared to have closed somewhat; the Reference area was composed of 22% of colonies in these classes, the Restored area 15%.

The inter-year density comparisons among the Orders in the Restored area proved interesting. Between 2005 and 2007, for Scleractinians there was a decrease, for Gorgonians an increase, though neither difference was found to be significant (this despite the fact that Gorgonian density rose 65% over the period, from 2.0 to 3.3 col./m²; the *p* value of the analysis was 0.0962). The only taxa to show a significant increase was the Milleporans which moved up from 0.7 to 1.7 col./m² (Figure 17).

Finally, the Reference area inter-year comparisons likewise proved interesting, but in a different fashion. The most noteworthy observation about the colony densities, across all Orders, is their remarkable consistency (Figure 18).

Overall, the *Elpis* restoration appeared to be relatively healthy, and doing well in comparison to adjacent reference areas. Despite a few unexplainable (or at least presently unexplained) anomalies referred to above, it is anticipated that, broadly speaking, general convergence to the reference conditions will continue. The next monitoring event is currently scheduled for

Summer 2010, and a follow-up report comparing data obtained in that year with the above will be prepared.

REFERENCES AND LITERATURE CITED

Adobe, Inc. 2002, 2005. Photoshop (image processing software), version 7; version CS2. www.adobe.com.

Bodge, K. and C. Creed, 1993. Conceptual Engineering Alternatives for Structural Restoration of the Maitland and Elpis Grounding Sites: Florida Keys National Marine Sanctuary. Report prepared for: Office of Ocean Resources Conservation and Assessment.

Bodge, K. 1994. Reef Restoration of the *M/V Alec Owen Maitland* and *M/V Elpis* Vessel Grounding Sites: Key Largo National Marine Sanctuary. Technical Specifications prepared for: National Oceanic and Atmospheric Administration.

Bodge, K. 1996. Engineering Summary Report: Structural Restoration of the *M/V Alec Owen Maitland* and *M/V Elpis* Vessel Grounding Sites: Florida Keys National Marine Sanctuary. Report prepared for: Office of Ocean Resources Conservation and Assessment.

Box, S.J. and P.J. Mumby. 2007. Effect of macroalgal competition on growth and survival of juvenile Caribbean corals. Marine Ecology Progress Series. 342: 139-149.

Gittings, S. 1991. Reef Coral Destruction at the M/V ELPIS Grounding Site, Key Largo National Marine Sanctuary.

GraphPad Software, Inc. 2003, 2007. InStat Instant Biostatistics, version 3.0; Prism 5 for Windows, version 5.00. www.graphpad.com.

Lang, J.C., H.R. Lasker, E.H. Gladfelter, P. Hallock, W.C. Jaap, F.J. Losada, and R.G. Muller. 1992. Spatial and Temporal Variability During Periods of Recovery after Mass Bleaching on Atlantic Coral Reefs. American Zoologist. 32:696-706.

Thayer, G. W. , T. A. McTigue, R. J. Bellmer, F. M. Burrows, D. H. Merkey, A. D. Nickens, S.J. Lozano, P. F. Gayaldo, P. J. Polmateer, and P. T. Pinit. 2003. Science-based restoration monitoring of coastal habitats, volume one: A framework for monitoring plans under the Estuaries and Clean Waters Act of 2000 (Public Law 160-457). NOAA Coastal Ocean Program Decision Analysis Series No.23, Volume 1. NOAA National Centers for Coastal Ocean Science, Silver Spring, MD. 35 pp. plus appendices.

APPENDIX

Comparative photographs of restoration boulders at the M/V *Elpis* grounding site from July 1997 (photo credits: Harold Hudson NMSP/NOAA.), August 2004, June 2005, and August 2007 (photo credits: Jeff Anderson NMSP/NOAA).

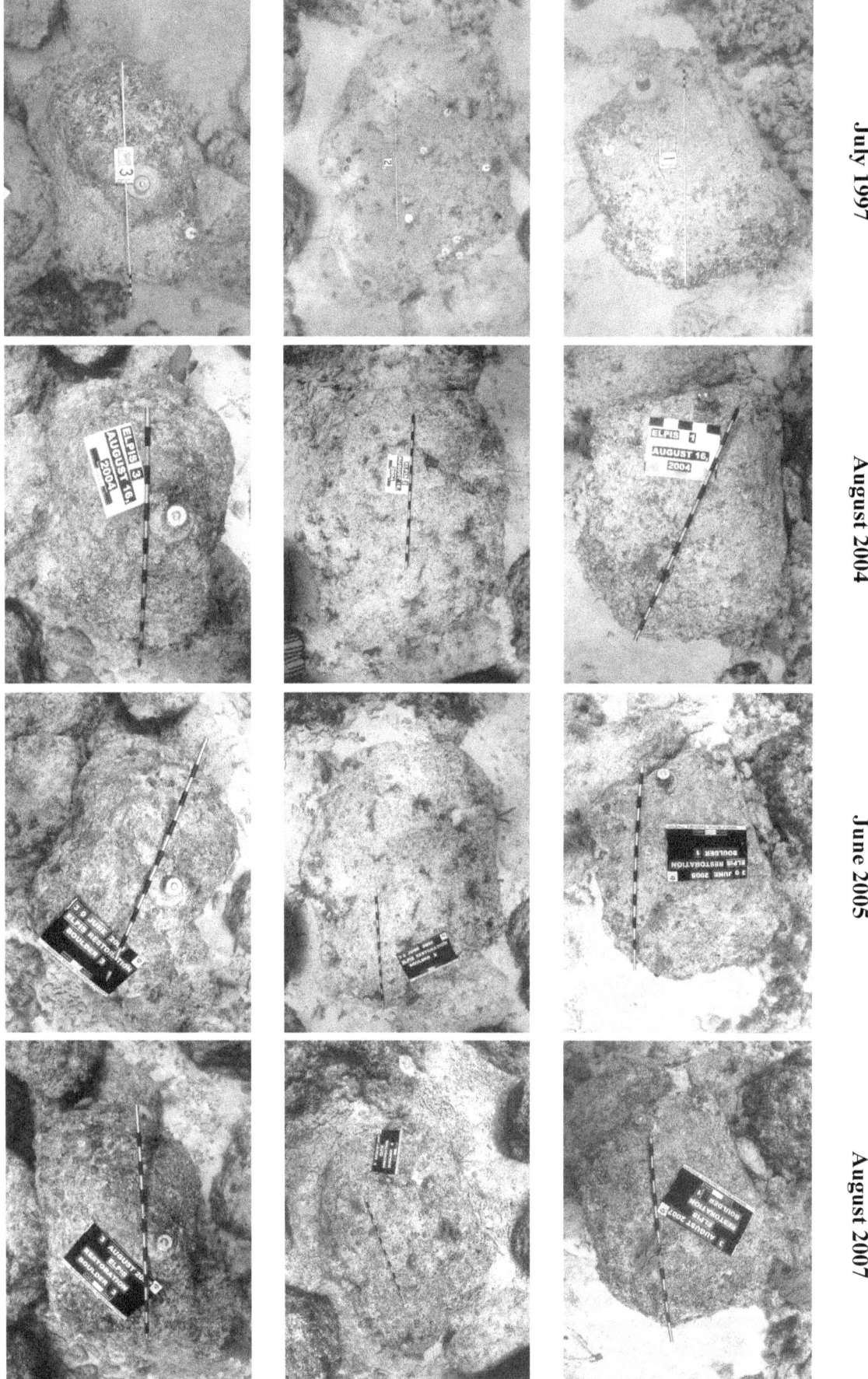

July 1997

August 2004

June 2005

August 2007

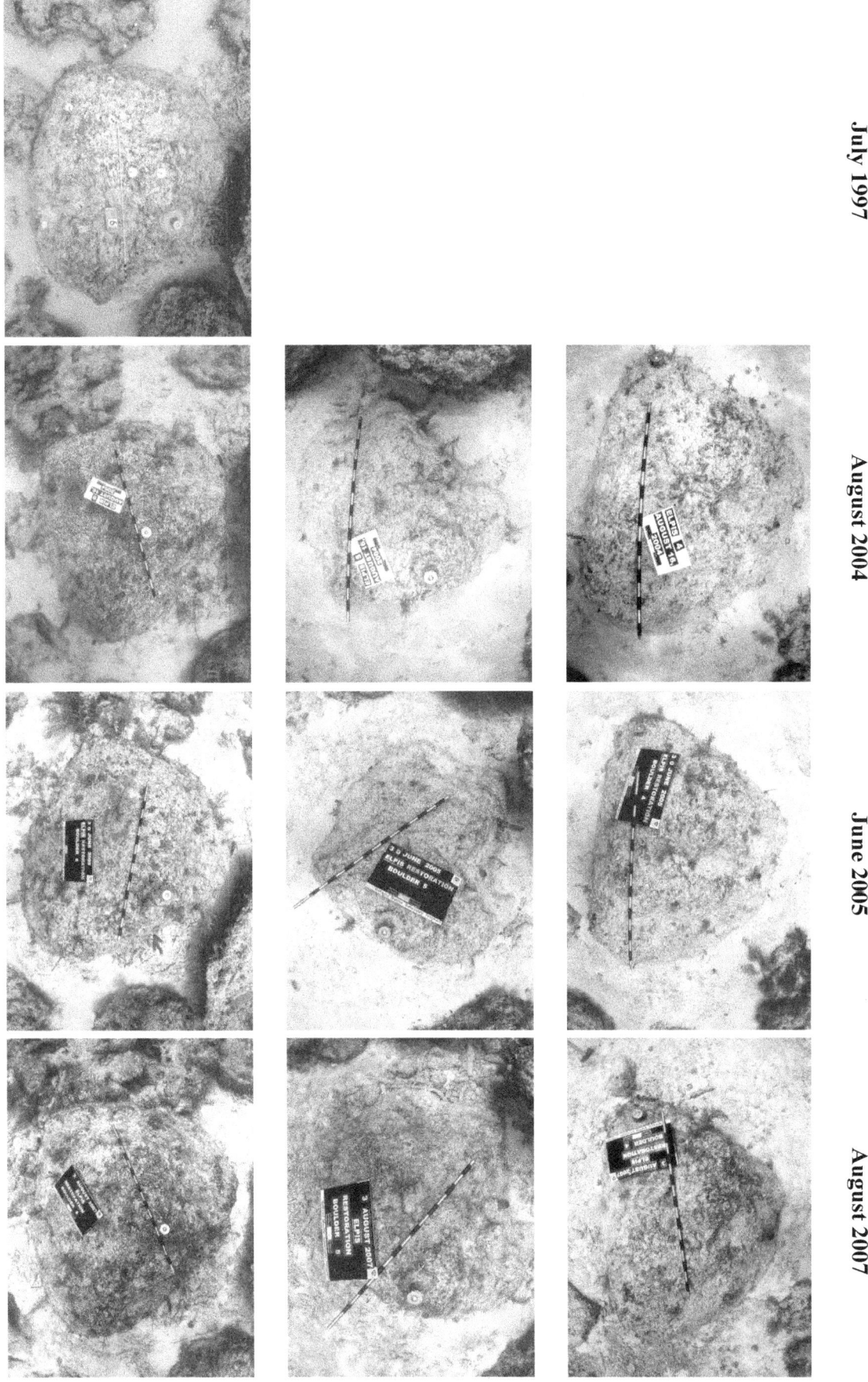

July 1997

August 2004

June 2005

August 2007

31

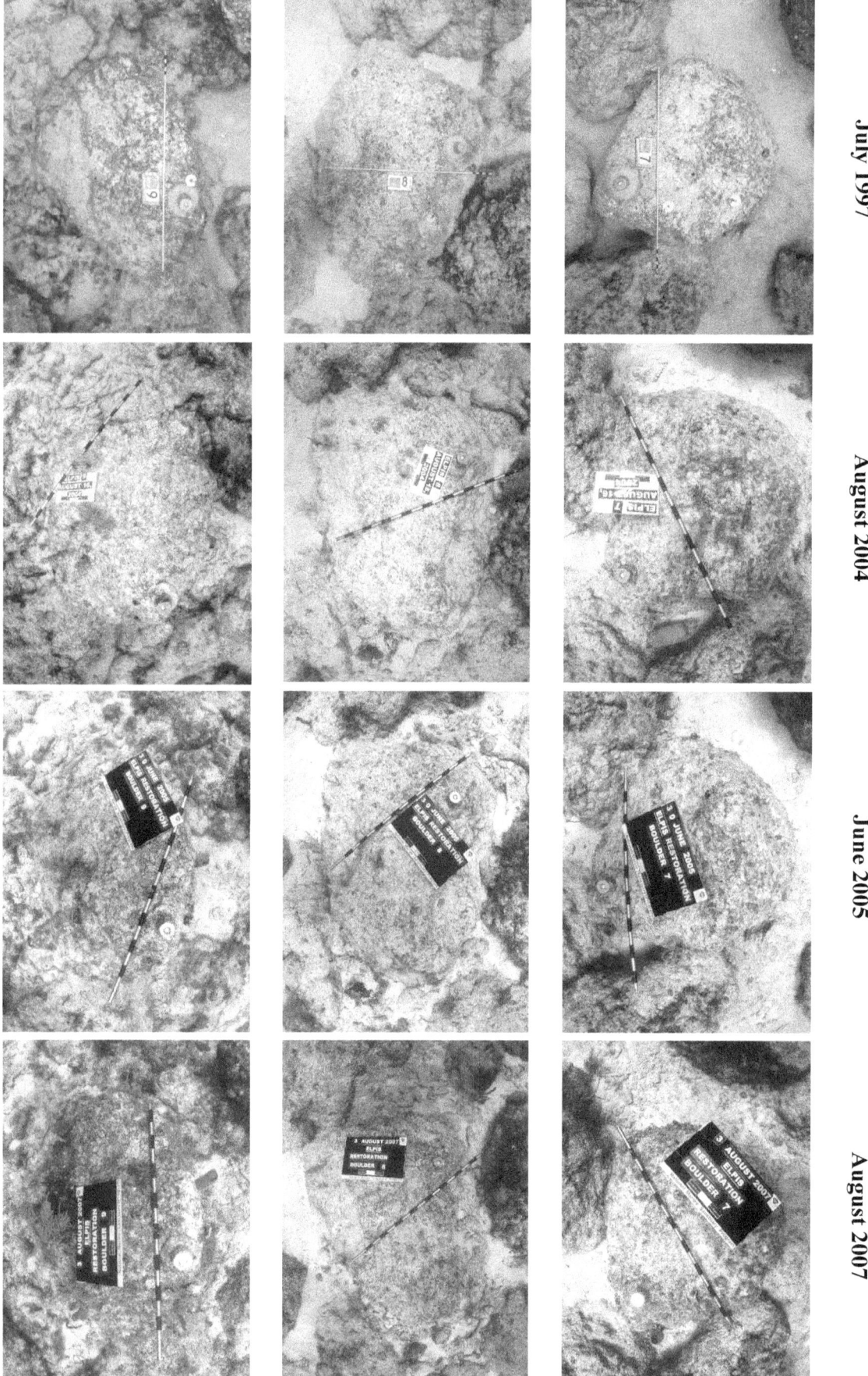

July 1997   August 2004   June 2005   August 2007

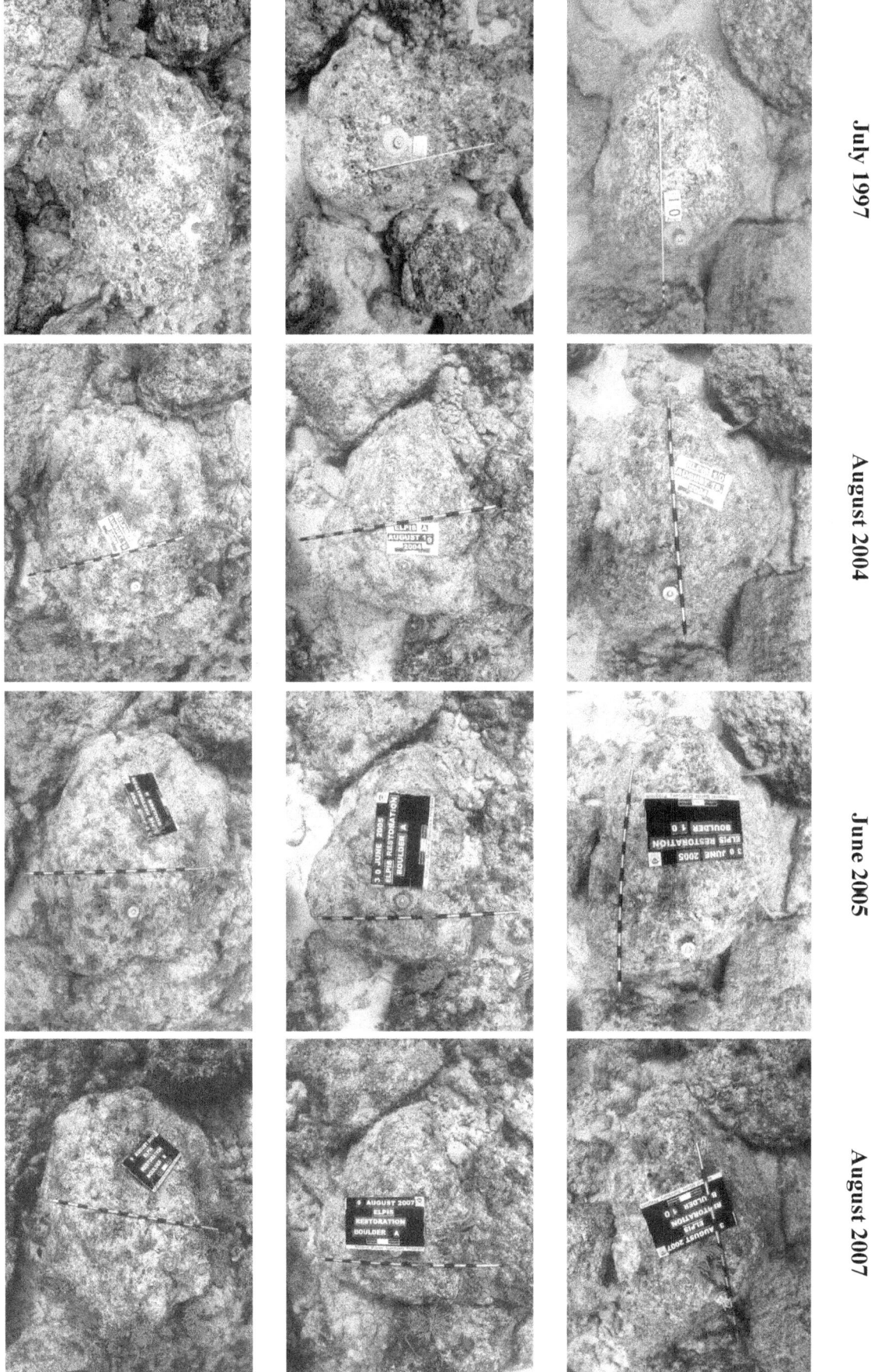

July 1997

August 2004

June 2005

August 2007

33

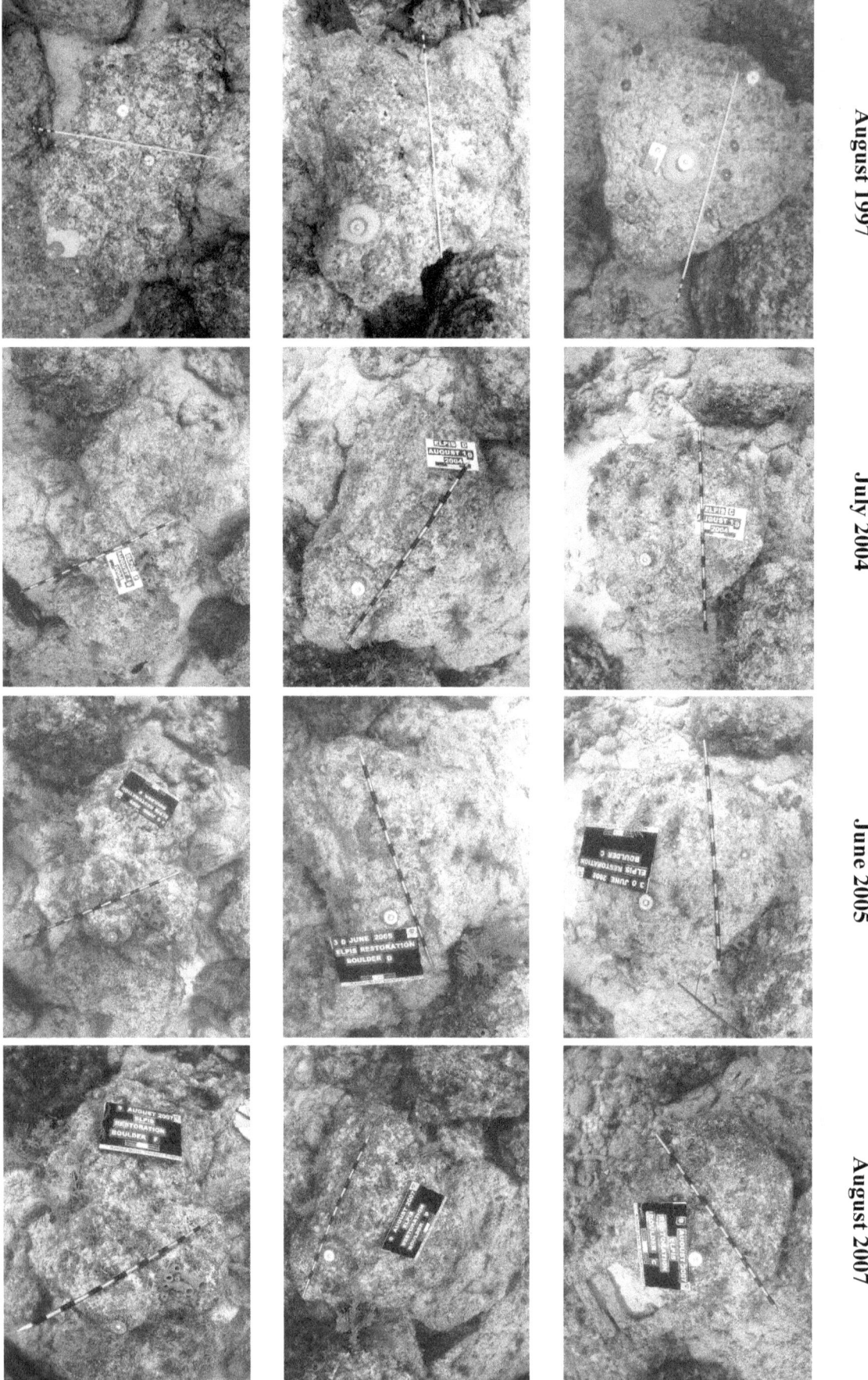

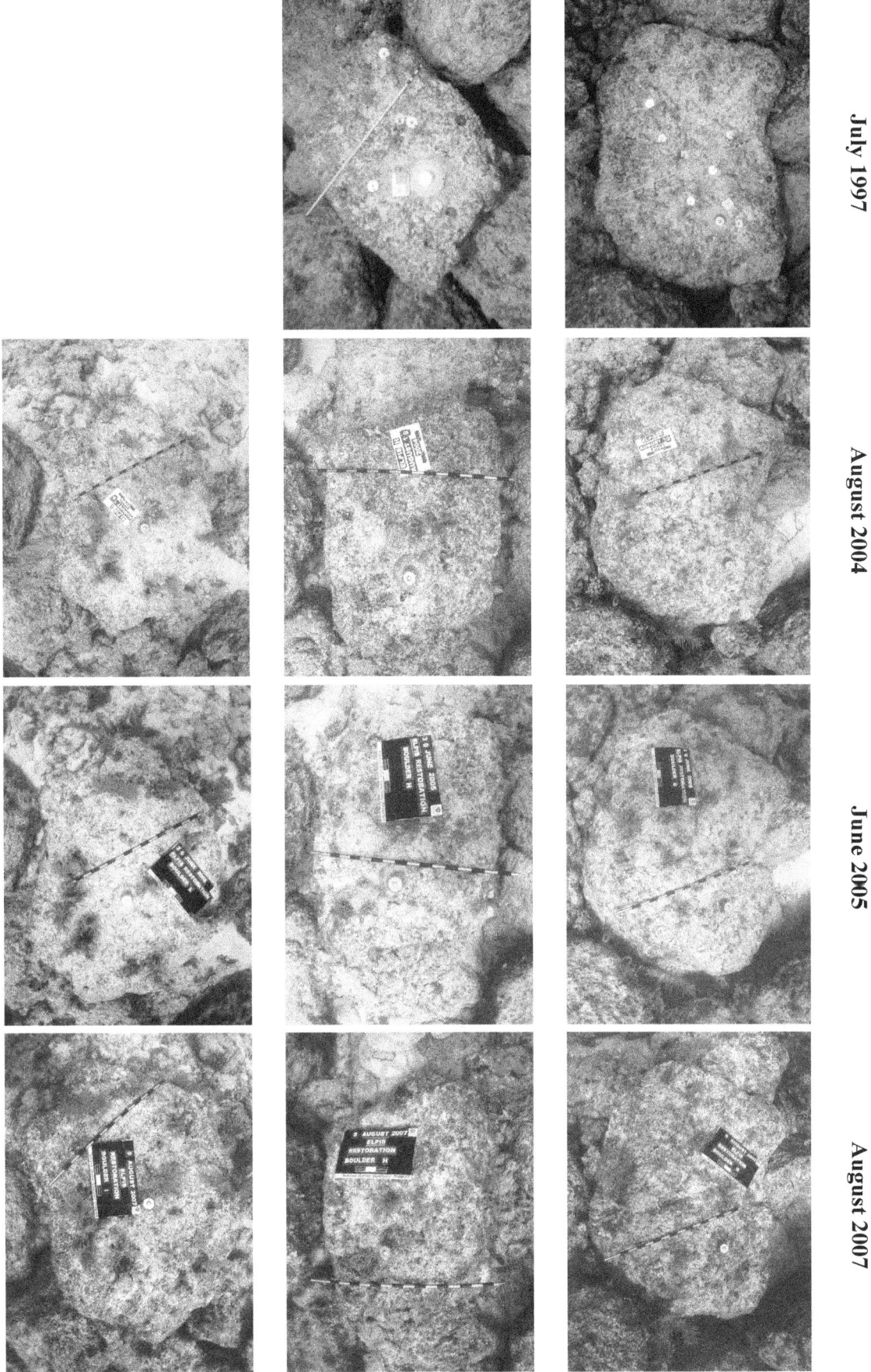

July 1997

August 2004

June 2005

August 2007

35

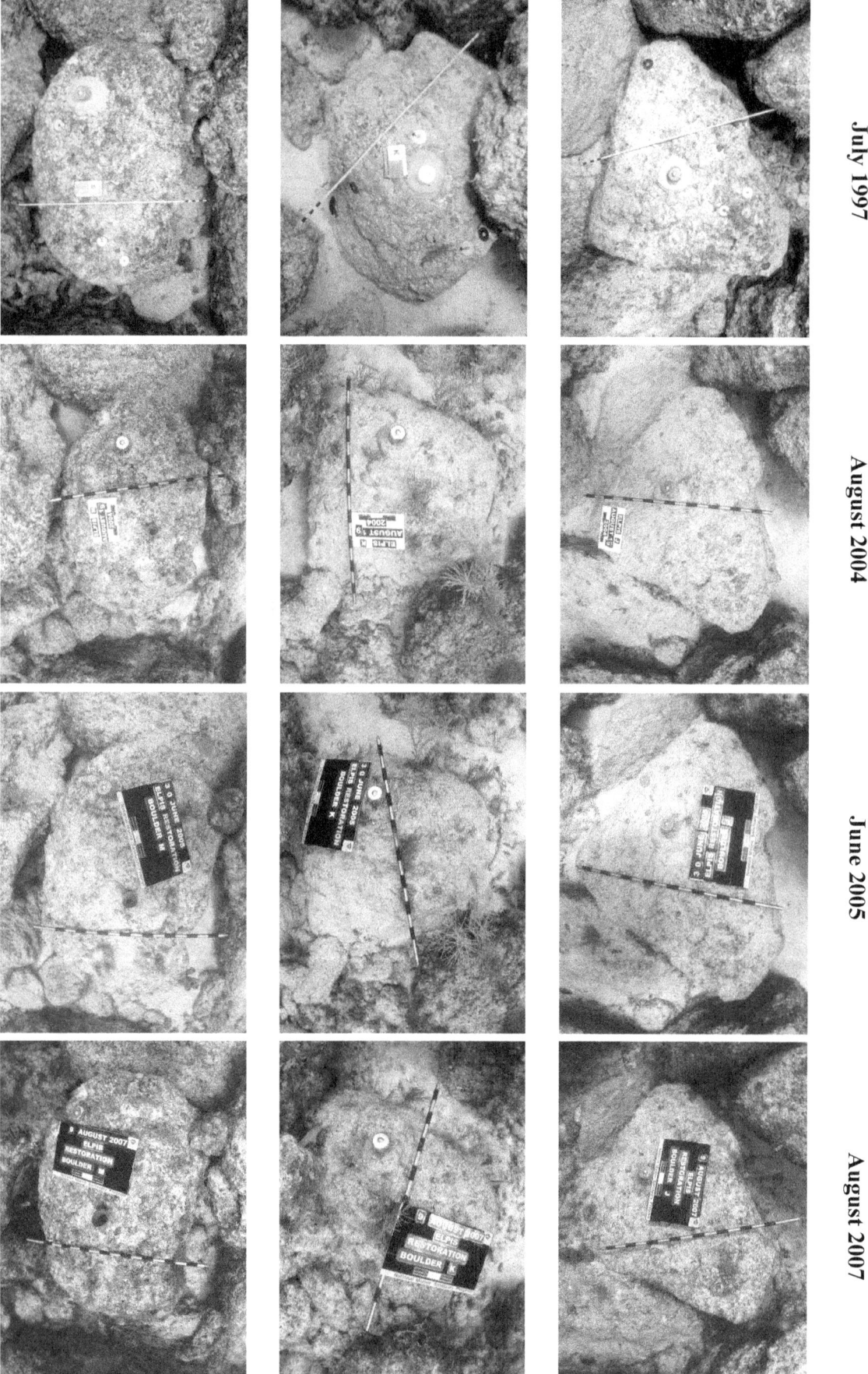

July 1997 August 2004 June 2005 August 2007

NMSP CONSERVATION SERIES PUBLICATIONS

To date, the following reports have been published in the Marine Sanctuaries Conservation Series. All publications are available on the National Marine Sanctuary Program website (http://www.sanctuaries.noaa.gov/).

CONNECTIVITY Science, People and Policy in the Florida Keys National Marine Sanctuary (NMSP-08-02)

M/V *ALEC OWEN MAITLAND* Coral Reef Restoration Monitoring Report Monitoring Events 2004-2007 Florida Keys National Marine Sanctuary Monroe County, Florida (NMSP-08-01)

Automated, objective texture segmentation of multibeam echosounder data - Seafloor survey and substrate maps from James Island to Ozette Lake, Washington Outer Coast. (NMSP-07-05)

Observations of Deep Coral and Sponge Assemblages in Olympic Coast National Marine Sanctuary, Washington (NMSP-07-04)

A Bioregional Classification of the Continental Shelf of Northeastern North America for Conservation Analysis and Planning Based on Representation (NMSP-07-03)

M/V *WELLWOOD* Coral Reef Restoration Monitoring Report Monitoring Events 2004-2006 Florida Keys National Marine Sanctuary Monroe County, Florida (NMSP-07-02)

Survey report of NOAA Ship McArthur II cruises AR-04-04, AR-05-05 and AR-06-03: Habitat classification of side scan sonar imagery in support of deep-sea coral/sponge explorations at the Olympic Coast National Marine Sanctuary (NMSP-07-01)

2002 - 03 Florida Keys National Marine Sanctuary Science Report: An Ecosystem Report Card After Five Years of Marine Zoning (NMSP-06-12)

Habitat Mapping Effort at the Olympic Coast National Marine Sanctuary - Current Status and Future Needs (NMSP-06-11)

M/V *CONNECTED* Coral Reef Restoration Monitoring Report Monitoring Events 2004-2005 Florida Keys National Marine Sanctuary Monroe County, Florida (NMSP-06-010)

M/V *JACQUELYN L* Coral Reef Restoration Monitoring Report Monitoring Events 2004-2005 Florida Keys National Marine Sanctuary Monroe County, Florida (NMSP-06-09)

M/V *WAVE WALKER* Coral Reef Restoration Baseline Monitoring Report - 2004 Florida Keys National Marine Sanctuary Monroe County, Florida (NMSP-06-08)

Olympic Coast National Marine Sanctuary Habitat Mapping: Survey report and classification of side scan sonar data from surveys HMPR-114-2004-02 and HMPR-116-2005-01 (NMSP-06-07)

A Pilot Study of Hogfish (*Lachnolaimus maximus* Walbaum 1792) Movement in the Conch Reef Research Only Area (Northern Florida Keys) (NMSP-06-06)

Comments on Hydrographic and Topographic LIDAR Acquisition and Merging with Multibeam Sounding Data Acquired in the Olympic Coast National Marine Sanctuary (ONMS-06-05)

Conservation Science in NOAA's National Marine Sanctuaries: Description and Recent Accomplishments (ONMS-06-04)

Normalization and characterization of multibeam backscatter: Koitlah Point to Point of the Arches, Olympic Coast National Marine Sanctuary - Survey HMPR-115-2004-03 (ONMS-06-03)

Developing Alternatives for Optimal Representation of Seafloor Habitats and Associated Communities in Stellwagen Bank National Marine Sanctuary (ONMS-06-02)

Benthic Habitat Mapping in the Olympic Coast National Marine Sanctuary (ONMS-06-01)

Channel Islands Deep Water Monitoring Plan Development Workshop Report (ONMS-05-05)

Movement of yellowtail snapper (Ocyurus chrysurus Block 1790) and black grouper (Mycteroperca bonaci Poey 1860) in the northern Florida Keys National Marine Sanctuary as determined by acoustic telemetry (MSD-05-4)

The Impacts of Coastal Protection Structures in California's Monterey Bay National Marine Sanctuary (MSD-05-3)

An annotated bibliography of diet studies of fish of the southeast United States and Gray's Reef National Marine Sanctuary (MSD-05-2)

Noise Levels and Sources in the Stellwagen Bank National Marine Sanctuary and the St. Lawrence River Estuary (MSD-05-1)

Biogeographic Analysis of the Tortugas Ecological Reserve (MSD-04-1)

A Review of the Ecological Effectiveness of Subtidal Marine Reserves in Central California (MSD-04-2, MSD-04-3)

Pre-Construction Coral Survey of the M/V Wellwood Grounding Site (MSD-03-1)

Olympic Coast National Marine Sanctuary: Proceedings of the 1998 Research Workshop, Seattle, Washington (MSD-01-04)

Workshop on Marine Mammal Research & Monitoring in the National Marine Sanctuaries (MSD-01-03)

A Review of Marine Zones in the Monterey Bay National Marine Sanctuary (MSD-01-2)

Distribution and Sighting Frequency of Reef Fishes in the Florida Keys National Marine Sanctuary (MSD-01-1)

Flower Garden Banks National Marine Sanctuary: A Rapid Assessment of Coral, Fish, and Algae Using the AGRRA Protocol (MSD-00-3)

The Economic Contribution of Whalewatching to Regional Economies: Perspectives From Two National Marine Sanctuaries (MSD-00-2)

Olympic Coast National Marine Sanctuary Area to be Avoided Education and Monitoring Program (MSD-00-1)

Multi-species and Multi-interest Management: an Ecosystem Approach to Market Squid (Loligo opalescens) Harvest in California (MSD-99-1)